My Walk with Mary

In the Footsteps of Bernadette

By Mary Marshall

PEAR TREE PUBLISHING

My Walk with Mary

In the Footsteps of Bernadette

Copyright © 2007 by Mary Marshall

Published by Pear Tree Publishing
PearTreePublishing@att.net

No part of this book may be reproduced in any form or by electronic or mechanical means including information storage and retrieval systems without permission in writing from the author, except in the case of brief quotations used in reviews. The views and opinions of the author do not necessarily reflect those of the Sovereign Military Hospitaller Order of St. John of Jerusalem of Rhodes and of Malta American Association, U.S.A. or any other parties mentioned in this book.

First Edition

Printed in the United States of America
By Signature Book Printing, Inc. Gaithersburg, MD

Marshall, Mary
    My Walk with Mary, In the Footsteps of Bernadette /
    by Mary Marshall – 1st Ed.

    ISBN 978-0-9749291-5-6
    Library of Congress Control Number: 2007932545

    1. Our Lady of Lourdes - Author. 2. Our Lady of Lourdes - Interpretation 3. Spiritualism
    I. Title II. Our Lady of Lourdes

Author's photograph by Patricia Axford
Cover & Book Design by Mary Marshall & Irene Bodkin
Cover Photo by Nova Development Corporation Copyright © 1995-98

Dedication

To Our Lady

and

*the fulfillment
of my promise
made long ago.*

Acknowledgements

The writing of this book was a labor of love. I believe that no one person really does anything alone. My life has been blessed with many wonderful people and to list them all would be impossible. So I will try to narrow the list to the people who were the most instrumental in helping me fulfill my dream.

Samarah, who started me on this journey. Thank you for sharing your beautiful gift with me and bringing the words and love of Mother Mary to the world.

Patricia Mullane, for your many years of friendship and your guidance regarding the Pilgrimage to Lourdes.

Jane Breault, for your listening ear, words of wisdom and enduring friendship.

Irene Bodkin, without whom this book would not have been completed. Thank you for your patience, dedication, hours of hard work, selflessness but most of all for your friendship.

St. Bernadette, who's Spirit has helped me to take back my Divine Power and who taught me by example to stand up for what I believe in, no matter what the consequences.

And finally, to Our Lady whose faith in me has never wavered. You have always been in my life and in my heart. Thank you for showing me the meaning of unconditional love.

Prologue

All the meetings were over, the planning sessions finished, and all the final details worked out. It was time to go. I'd done this many times before so I had a pretty good idea what to expect. I just wanted one more look around and another chance to say good-bye and thanks to everyone for their love, guidance and support.

"I think I'm ready."

"We know you are."

"Thanks again for everything. You've always been here for me through thick and thin. I don't know what I would do without all of You."

"We love you. We always have and We always will."

"All right, I know the plan. I've gone over it a thousand times. I know what my name is, who my parents and siblings are, where I'm going to live, who I'm going to meet and most importantly, what I am supposed to do. Don't worry, this time I won't forget."

"You must forget. That is the way it works."

"But I can't forget this time. It's too important."

"Oh, you will remember for a time. A few years perhaps, maybe more, but then the memories will start to fade. At times there will be moments of clarity, maybe a spark of recognition, but this too in time will pass. There will be times when you feel that it is all too hard and you cannot go on. Then there will be times when you feel Us so close that you could almost see and touch Us. But you will always know deep in the memory of your heart that We would never leave or forsake you."

"But I can't forget. The reason why I am doing this again is because I didn't get it quite right the last time. What is the purpose of going back down again if I can't remember why I am there in the first place?"

"All right, don't get upset. We will add a clause to your contract. At exactly the right time, We will arrange a meeting for you to be introduced to someone who will help you start to remember. You will recognize her immediately, don't worry."

"So, You're saying that this time I will accomplish my goal? I will remind everyone who they really are?"

"That is up to you."

"What? You said…but wait a minute…"

"Congratulations, it's a girl!"

.   .   .   .

What is going on? Why is it so noisy? Why am I so cold? And why do I feel like I have been stuffed inside a football? Oh yeah, that's right. I remember.

As the weeks and months went by the little girl remained connected to her Source. She was being loved and cared for on the outside while still experiencing that feeling of "home" on the inside. Her parents would talk baby talk to her, while her teachers and guides would communicate the wisdom of the ages, and she would say, "I remember."

When she became a toddler and went for walks in the park with her parents, the birds would sing to her and she would understand every word.

As she grew older and started playing with dolls, there would be a few "extra" friends at the tea parties and she would proudly say to them, "See, I told You. I still remember".

She was a very happy child. She loved going for walks and talking to all the birds and flowers and trees. She enjoyed her tea parties and was always excited to see who would come. She loved going to bed at night because she always had such sweet dreams of "home."

When the little girl started school, she could not have been happier. She made many new friends and was keeping very busy. She loved her new teachers. She was learning so much about the world around her.

As she grew and became more active in school activities, she realized there wasn't as much time for tea parties anymore. But that was all right, she thought to herself. Tea parties are just for children, anyway.

One day, when she was walking home from school, she took a shortcut through the park. It was a beautiful, warm and sunny spring day. As she was walking, she noticed a Robin's nest in a nearby tree. Full of excitement, she ran over to see the little birds. As she stood there under the nest, she began to cry.

By the time she arrived home, she had stopped crying but her mother could tell she was very upset. When her mother asked what was wrong and tried to comfort her, the little girl just ran to her room.

When she didn't come down for dinner, her mother went up to her room and saw that she was already in bed.

"What's wrong, honey?" her mother asked. The little girl looked up with such sadness in her eyes it almost broke her mothers heart. "I couldn't hear them," the little girl said.

"Hear who, honey?" her mother asked, a bit confused.

"The robins. I couldn't hear them." As her mother put her arms around her daughter, the little girl stared out the window and asked, "Do you really want to know why I am so sad, mommy?" Her mother nodded and waited for her answer. "It's because I'm starting to forget."

"I don't understand honey," her mother said. "Forget what?" Still staring out the window, the little girl replied, "I'm starting to forget who I am."

Chapter I

Think back to when you were young, to when life was simple. Summer days seemed to last forever and Christmas was so magical it took your breath away. Were you too busy having fun to even think of tomorrow? Who took the magic away? Or maybe a more accurate question would be, why did you let them?

Little by little, day by day, the world takes hold of us and we slowly start to forget our connection to our Source. We start to forget who we really are. We learn what to say and whom it is safe to say it to. We are taught by our parents what is appropriate, by our schools how to think, and by our Churches what to believe. We start to lose our original truth. We start to conform. Is it so subtle that we don't even realize it's happening? Or do we simply resign ourselves to the fact that we have no choice?

Imagine that you had the power to go back and change any part of your life. If you had the chance to do it all over again, what would you do differently? It is a powerful thought. Was there one dream that you had that was so personal, so intimate to your very core that you never shared it with anyone? What if that dream suddenly unfolded before your very eyes. What if I told you it wasn't too late?

We are all here to make our dreams come true, to bring heaven home. We each have a complete, pristine and beautiful gift to give to the world. We are each a piece of a patchwork quilt. We are all here for a reason. Our stories may be different but we are all searching for our own truth.

I believe that if you are reading these words you are on your own personal spiritual journey. A journey that may have started yesterday or one you have been traveling for years. A road we ultimately travel alone but certainly not without assistance.

It is time to take back your power. It is never too late. Stop giving yourself away in bits and pieces. I asked you to imagine what you would do if you had the power to go back and change any part of your life. Now I want you to think about what you can change right now. What is stopping you? You've known for a while that it is time for things to change. Let your knowing break through your fear. Let it guide you. Say yes to all your opportunities. When you say yes, miracles happen.

I invite you to come with me as I try to reclaim my truth. Watch what can happen when you listen to that small, still voice inside your head, set aside your fears and say, "Yes," to life. In doing so, you can experience with me the incredible gift I received along the way. It is my fondest wish through reading my story you will be able to remember who *you* really are.

When I was a small child, around the age of five, something extraordinary happened to me something that has shaped and influenced my life to this day.

I was alone playing in my living room. My parents were at work and my older sisters and brother were in school. My aunt, who lived with us, was in the bathroom washing something out in the sink. As I was entertaining myself by playing with some imaginary friends, I heard the most beautiful and gentle voice say, "Hello Mary." The voice filled the room, though it seemed to have come from no particular place. I knew at once that it was God. Frightened, I ran to my aunt. She didn't even notice me, as she was still busy with her wash. I knew she hadn't heard the voice however, because deep down I understood that it was meant just for me.

I kept this to myself for a long time, never telling my parents or my siblings. It wasn't until the first day of school that I decided to share this news with a friend. As we were walking to school, I just came right out and told her that God had talked to me. She laughed so hard that I never mentioned it again to anyone for the next twenty years. As the years went on, I often wondered when or if I would ever hear that voice again.

All my life I've felt that there was something extremely important I was not being told. Some really big secret that God was keeping from me until the time was right, until I was ready to hear it.

Well, on June 9, 2004 God decided it was time to let me in on that secret. Never in my wildest dreams could I have imagined the gift that was waiting for me to unwrap.

We all enter this world with a sacred contract. Each one of us has a plan. We all incarnate with a certain goal in mind. We are here for a purpose. The trick is trying to remember it. Some people go through life without a clue, while others find their way at a very early age. After many years of soul searching, I can now, without a doubt, state that I remember.

I am about to tell you a story that some may find hard to believe. My intent is not to convince you of its validity, but to simply tell you of my experience.

This book is not meant to criticize any one religion, although in reading it some may be offended. This is not my purpose nor intent. This is a story about two people sharing the same soul. Two very ordinary people. Ordinary, until their lives drastically change by an encounter with the Divine.

Some of you may not believe what you are about to read, and that's all right. My hope is that in the telling of my experience you may be able to accept your own.

I have lived in New England all of my life. I am the youngest of four children born to blue-collar workers. My father was a proofreader for a printing company and my mother worked in a department store. I would have loved it if my mother stayed at home, but she needed to feel useful outside the home.

When my parents were at work, my aunt, one of mother's sisters who never married, cared for us. We loved her very much. She was like a second mother to us. My grandparents died before I was born and I always regretted never getting to meet them. Old photographs and passed down stories were all I had of them.

Growing up, we didn't have a lot of money. We did not even own a car until my oldest sister got her license.

I was what you would call a tomboy. My brother was only twenty-two months older than me and I shadowed him. Instead of playing with dolls, I played baseball and football. We did just about everything together.

My oldest sister was eight years my senior, and at a young age, that seemed like worlds apart. My other sister was only four years older, but that still made me young enough to be a pest.

We took one family vacation a year, spending two weeks at Hampton Beach, New Hampshire. We started going before I was even a year old. What an ordeal it was for my parents to get us there. We didn't have a car, so they had to ask a neighbor or a relative to drive us. I think, if she had to, my mother would have carried us all on her back. She lived for those two weeks. I never saw her happier than when she was at the beach.

By the time I came along, my parents marriage was a little shaky and at thirty-seven, the last thing my mother wanted was another baby. I always heard stories that she said a novena to the Blessed Mother praying that she wasn't pregnant. Later in life I found out that it was true, although my father always denied it.

My mother stayed home with me until I started school. I didn't go to kindergarten, but went right into first grade and I will never forget my first day of school. When my mother dropped me off and started to leave I began to cry. I must have made quite a scene, because she reassured me that she wasn't really leaving, that she would be waiting for me right outside the door. When the nun took me by the hand and tried to seat me at my desk, I quickly opened the door to find my mother gone. I felt abandoned. I screamed so loud that all the other kids started making fun of me. The sister looked me sternly in the eyes and said that if I did not stop she would sit me over with the boys. I was there for days. I don't think I ever got over that feeling of abandonment.

The other thing that I will never forget is the sound of my parents fighting. They fought mostly behind closed doors. I suppose they felt less guilty that way. I remember when my father would emerge after a go-around. I would sit him in a chair and comb his hair or try in some way to make him look better so maybe my mother would love him more. It didn't work.

I can't pinpoint the exact time when things started getting worse but it was around the time we moved. I was eleven, and leaving all my friends was hard enough, but starting a new school at that age was torture. I was entering the sixth grade and my brother the eighth. We didn't exactly blend right in. School started a few days before we moved, so we had to take a cab. We disembarked right in the middle of the schoolyard amidst glaring stares. The first week of school we didn't have to wear uniforms. I really didn't have any good clothes, so my mother bought me a new skirt, blouse and sweater. I wore that outfit all week and everyone was laughing at me behind my back. Children can be so cruel. I was so upset that I would pretend I was sick so I could stay home. My mother let me get away with if for a few days. I finally started making a few neighborhood friends who attended the same school, so I began to feel like I fit in. Both my brother and I adjusted. My older sister met new friends in high school and my oldest sister was in college and dating the man she would end up marrying.

I think the pressures of a new house and a new position at work, with more responsibilities, was too much for my mother to handle. My father was a great guy, but he never had much ambition. He would go to work, come home, and sit in front of the television with a beer. This infuriated my mother. She wanted him to be someone with drive, someone who would take charge, someone who would take care of her, someone he was not and never would be.

It was around this time that we stopped going away for our two weeks to the beach. It was also the same time that I started to find empty whiskey bottles hidden around the house. The next few years were very sad ones. My mother was an alcoholic but no one was doing anything about it. No one even talked about it. I can remember one Christmas Eve waiting for my mother to come home from work. I was so excited because this was the first time I was being allowed to go to Midnight Mass. I'll never forget watching my mother being helped up the stairs to her room by two of her friends from work and then slump into bed, too out of it to even notice me. Shortly after that she lost her job.

One month before my fifteenth birthday, my mother died unexpectedly. She was only fifty-one. We were all devastated. I think it hit my oldest sister the hardest because she was in the midst of making her wedding plans. Her wedding was only four months away. The family convinced her not to change her plans, so the wedding went on, but it was bittersweet. As the months went on, we all tried to put the pieces of our lives back together. You just seem to go through the motions and time passes. I don't think my father ever got over my mother's death. He never remarried.

His drinking got a little heavier and his mood more somber. He was very lonely. I regret not spending more time with him, but I was young and my own life was unfolding. Now, with only my father's income, the possibility of having to sell our house was very real. By this time, I was a little less than two months away from entering my sophomore year in high school. Although I went to what you would consider a private school, the tuition was minimal. It was an all girls school and I had made many good friends my first year. When my father asked me if I would drop out and go to our public school because of finances, I cried. Realizing how much I had already lost, he let me stay. I loved high school. I lived in walking distance and when classes were over for the day, there would be a group of us that would stay and hang out with the nuns. We never wanted to leave. There comes a point in the lives of some young, Catholic girls when they consider entering the convent. I was no exception. Although it was brief, there was a time when I thought about becoming a nun. For me, I think it was just a phase but there were a lot of girls who did make that decision. In the long run, I decided there would be too many restrictions.

All through Catholic school I was taught from the Baltimore Catechism. In it, there were specific questions with specific answers. There was no room for doubt. We all believed whole-heartedly in the information that was handed to us because we all had "faith."

Faith can be a funny thing. Do we have faith in something because deep down in our gut we truly believe or do we have faith because it's what we were told to believe?

To be fair, the people who taught us from the Baltimore Catechism fervently believed every word of it. And so did I, at the time.

However, there comes a time when you have to look outside the box. Going outside the box can be scary. It's comfortable in the box. It's familiar. It's safe. What might happen if we started questioning what we were taught by our parents and the Church?

I started breaking out of the box at around eighteen. My brother and sisters were all out of the house by then. I stayed at home to take care of my father and my aunt.

I decided in my junior year of high school that I was not going to college. There were a few reasons for that decision. At that time, when a woman was entering college she was going to get a degree in either nursing or education. I wanted neither. I wasn't exactly an "A" student and I was getting tired of school. But to be really honest, I didn't think I was smart enough. Looking back now, I realize that I probably could have succeeded very well in school but at eighteen I didn't have much academic confidence. Besides, I told myself that if I got a job, I could help my father out with the bills. I eventually took over the running of the house, much to my father's relief. A friend of mine knew of an opening in a doctor's office and believe it or not, I have been there ever since.

Up until my mother died, we all pretty much followed the rules. Church on Sunday and Holy Days of Obligation. Confession at least once a month and, of course, no meat on Fridays. I can't speak for the rest of my family, but I can honestly say that I followed the rules until I graduated from high school. I didn't want to go to hell!

I can't say exactly when I started missing Mass, but it probably had a lot to do with my brand new 1970 Ford Maverick. Why drive to Church when my friends and I could go on a really nice ride? Of course, I was home at around the same time Mass would be getting out. Although I must say, my father and aunt were very trusting, and with good reason, as I never got into any trouble.

I did have some guilt about not going to Church, but my ideas of hell were beginning to change. My beliefs were starting to change, but my love for God just grew stronger. How could a God who spoke so lovingly to me have anything but love for me, whether I went to Church or not, or even if I was starting to question everything I had been taught? And I was. I have since learned that guilt is a useless emotion, but I think Catholics were brought up on it. Who did I think I was to question the beliefs I had held all my life? What would people think if I told them that the concept of reincarnation was starting to make sense to me? Believe me, my transformation didn't happen overnight. Little by little, year after year, I allowed myself to look at things differently. I think too many times we live our lives to please other people. I think that is true for women especially. As a young adult I was just trying to fit in. Speaking about your spiritual beliefs back then was not really "in." So, for a very long time, I was a closet New Ager. After years of keeping my changing ideas to myself, I slowly started voicing my thoughts to some of my friends. As much as they loved me, they all thought I was nuts. I didn't care, because I knew that I was on to something.

I've always felt a special bond with the Blessed Mother. I knew my mother named me Mary for a reason. I was always picked to be Mary in the May processions and when the nuns would ask us to come to school dressed as our favorite saint, my mother would dress me in a blue dress and a blue veil with rosary beads in my hands.

I knew Mary would understand all the questions I had about what I was brought up to believe. I knew she was standing right beside me smiling.

It was around that time that I came across a book by Jane Roberts. I wasn't a great reader at the time, but I finished her book in just days.

Jane Roberts was born in 1929. She channeled an entity known as Seth. Another well-known channeler was Edgar Cayce. Channeling is the act of an entity or spirit literally speaking through someone. The Old Testament is full of examples of channeling, starting with Moses, followed by Solomon, Samuel, Daniel, Elijah, Ezekiel and Isaiah. In the New Testament, Jesus was a channel of God Himself.

After reading Jane Roberts book, I was hooked. I believe that nothing in our lives happens by accident. Little did I realize then what a life-changing effect channeling would have on my life some thirty years later.

Looking back now, I can see that I was being prepared for my revelation. I always knew that there was someone or someplace that would give me the answers to all of my questions. Questions like, why did God speak to me in such a profound way? Why did I feel that there was something very important I was supposed to share with the world, but couldn't figure out what it was? And why did I feel such a profound connection to Jesus and the Blessed Mother?

I looked in a lot of places for those answers. After many years away from the Church, I decided to return to Sunday Mass. But as hard as I tried, I realized that I could honor God just as well on my own, without having to be in a building, so I stopped attending again. I was one of those Catholics who only saw the inside of a Church on Christmas and Easter.

Don't get me wrong, my love for God never wavered. I believe religion and spirituality are two different things. I had a prayer life, it just wasn't a formal one. Though I didn't sit down each day and recite the Rosary, I was in constant communication with God in one way or another.

My father died when I was twenty-nine. I think that no matter how old you are it's very traumatic when one of your parents dies. I had never married, so I was still at home sharing the house with my aunt. We always got along very well, to the day she died at the age of eighty-two.

When I was in my early thirties, a close friend of mine asked if I would like to join a prayer group with her. By this time, I was calling myself a "recovering Catholic," but I agreed to go. I met a lot of very lovely people. I became close friends with another single woman in the group and when her mother passed away, we decided to share expenses and become housemates. I stayed with the prayer group for a few years, but a lot of what I felt differed from their beliefs, so I gracefully bowed out.

When a metaphysical bookstore opened close to my home, I was thrilled. I think I bought nearly every book in the store. Each one was insightful and thought provoking, but there still seemed to be something missing. I knew there was something else that I was meant to know.

I started seeing psychics, in the hope that they could give me the answers I was looking for. Though they were all very good, I still wasn't satisfied.

In addition to selling books and other items, the bookstore also welcomed outside guests. It offered various workshops, card readings, psychic readings and yes, people who channel.

The first person I met with channeled Ascended Masters. He was wonderful. He confirmed the fact that I did have a past life at the time of Jesus, something that I had always felt. He also told me that the voice I heard as a child was that of St. Germain. In another incarnation, St. Germain was Joseph, the husband of Mary and father to Jesus. He told me we were working very closely in this lifetime.

After I left that session, I was flying high. Had I finally found my answers? Was it because I had lived a life with the Holy Family that I felt so connected to them? I convinced myself that I had finally found the lost pieces of the puzzle. Although the aching in my heart eased up, I was still looking for ways to deepen my commitment to my spiritual growth.

I have long been fascinated with the mind, body, spirit connection. Several years earlier I had become a Reiki Master. I loved doing energy work. It further connected me with my spirit guides. During the final phase of my training, I realized that the Blessed Mother was working with me. I wasn't too surprised. After becoming a Reiki Master, I became a licensed massage therapist and finally a certified hypnotherapist, all the while still working in the doctor's office.

I continued to frequent my favorite bookstore. I was involved in many workshops and would read anything and everything that was put on the shelves. The owner of the bookstore would send out quarterly newsletters with information regarding new books and upcoming events. I always looked forward to these newsletters, eager to learn anything new. Whenever it arrived, I always scanned through it before opening any of my other mail.

The 2004 winter edition proved to be very exciting. There was a woman called Samarah from Arizona who channeled Mother Mary. The Mother of Jesus is known by many names: the Virgin Mary, the Lady of Light, the Blessed Mother, Mother Mary, the Queen of Heaven and the Mother of God, to name just a few. I desperately wanted to make an appointment, but I really disliked driving in the winter and Samarah was booked in February. I said to God, if it were really meant for me to see this woman then she would have to come in better weather. Well, as it turned out, she had to cancel her February plans and she rescheduled for June. I quickly made an appointment.

In the next chapter I will recount for you word for word the messages I received from Mother Mary. As you will see, the information took me by surprise at first but as I sat there in the energy of Our Lady, I knew without a doubt that this was the beginning of my awakening.

Chapter II

The morning of June 9, 2004 started off like any other day, but it was evident by the end of the day that my life would never be the same again. It was Wednesday and I had a half-day at work, as always. I was excited because this was the day I was to see the woman who channeled the Blessed Mother. I started to prepare by writing down all my questions, questions about work, finance, health, relationships, and the usual things anyone would ask. But as you will see, my list went out the window halfway through the session.

    As I always do, I arrived early for my appointment. I would rather be a half an hour early than be one single minute late. Samarah was still in with a client, so I browsed through the store, something I love to do anyway. As I waited for my turn, my excitement was building. I looked at a few books, not really reading any one of them.

    Then Samarah came into the room and introduced herself to me. She said that she would need just a few more minutes and that she would come back for me when she was ready. After a brief time, she returned, gesturing for me to follow her upstairs.

The room was warm and inviting. I had been in it several times before for workshops, classes and other readings. I was a little nervous at first, but after talking with her for just a few minutes, I felt completely at ease. Samarah made you feel right at home. After a few minutes of small talk, she asked me if I had any questions about what we were about to do. I said I didn't and she began to prepare.

Samarah started by asking that we be surrounded by the Holy Light of Father/Mother God. She asked that the angels, guides and teachers who work with each one of us draw near, and that the over lighting angels, that are here at all times, spread their wings of courage, compassion, loyalty and love over us. She welcomed and invited all of the archangels, Michael, Gabriel, Uriel and Rafael. She thanked them for joining us and for sharing their generosity, wisdom and love. Then she invited and invoked the presence of Mother Mary. She asked to be a clear channel for her information and for all that was spoken to be of the highest good for the receiver, herself and all beings everywhere. After a moment of centering she started.

The following is the message I received from Mother Mary. She speaks first.

"I want to say hello. I feel like I'm saying hello to an old friend."

"I hope so."

"Yes, you and I have had many walks together."

"So I've heard."

"Oh, you don't remember yet?"

"I'm trying to remember. I wonder if you could help me."

"Certainly, but before I do that I am going to make a suggestion, if that is all right? There are certain places in the world where I am felt more than in other places. There is a place called Lourdes in the south of France, and I think that if you were ever to go there, there would be not only a memory, but also some experiences that would be very profound for you. I do not often suggest this to people. I want you to know that. Know that you do not have to go there to feel me, but there is a recollection that could occur there. Like peeling away an onion, some of the layers of this life are dispelled so that you can remember not only this life but also many others. There are stories there for you. For you, there is a physical hunger that you will experience in your body. And I think no matter what I tell you or others tell you…it is as though your body wants to remember and this is why some places cause a palpable experience where I believe you could remember very clearly in the way you are trying to remember. You do not want to remember with your mind, but with your heart and your body, in a place where so many have gone and threaded themselves into the history of how I first came to Bernadette. Like I said, there would be a palpable experience for you there and I believe that is what your body wants before your mind and body can be at peace with this. Right now, many have told you things and in your mind you're saying, 'Well, yes but…' and I say that is all right. There is nothing wrong with being skeptical. There is nothing wrong with using discernment. It is important to not be taken in by information, because when you feel something, no one can tell you otherwise. This is what you seek. You seek to feel, and so you will.

"I would like to tell you a few things if that is all right? Part of the reason you have difficulty in this life from time to time is because you've known other lives where you didn't have a body and yet you had a presence here on the earth that was very, very important. And you acted in a way, let's find a word, you have so many different words for things. Well, I think you would call it the little divas in the garden. I think that's the easiest way. When most people think of divas, they think of something not very grand and yet you were quite grand. If you would ever like to read a little about Findhorn in Scotland, you would find out a little more about the importance of the divic kingdom and what took place there. Years ago, when they listened to the divic kingdom, they were able to grow in the soil of Scotland magnificent rose bushes, beautiful, beautiful pumpkins and squash and things that normally would not be grown there. It was because they were able to interact with the divic kingdom that they could do this.

"You dwelled on the earth in a divic capacity, assisting those who were sensitive to bring forth from the earth a great bounty. And this was done in around 1200 to 1400, as your earth knows time. You found this work very satisfying because you helped people to go from a place of always looking to find meat to eat for the next day to learning how to grow things in the earth and be able to stay in one place and have a beautiful garden and have things to eat. It was quite lovely. And then you decided you really wanted some other experiences because that was about the time in which they began to have this idea that you had peasants and you had the lords of the manor and all of that and you really couldn't stand that at all. You really weren't happy with that because it took away the joy of being part of the growing of the earth.

"After this, you had several lives as a person who tried to equalize rights. I guess that would be the easiest way to say it. You always came to talk about equality and to help those less fortunate find their way in life. You were not afraid to speak out to those who abused their power. You were killed at various times and in various ways that were not always pleasant. In your present life you have a great love of equality. You still speak out, yet there has been a certain reluctance partly because of the consequences you faced in previous lives.

"Part of the reason you are here today and that you want proof is that you know this life is different. You know that someone isn't going to come cart you off to prison or chop off your head or pull you apart on a wheel, all those terrible things that have happened in the past. Yet in a way you have been waiting for a sign to absolutely prove to yourself that now is the right time, the right place and that you are the right person to do whatever you feel that you need to do. You have looked in many places for this sign. I want to tell you that although you will not get it from me today I believe that it will come very soon. It should not come from me in this way, but should come absolutely from your own experience. Almost, dare I say, with a sense of serendipity, unexpected in a way. If you decide to go to Lourdes, for instance, it is important that you not have any expectations, but simply to go and say, 'I'm going to France. Let me go and just see what happens.'

"The difficulty of going somewhere to have an experience is that you want it so much and you end up pushing it away. So if you decide to go, just say to yourself, 'Oh, I'm going on holiday,' and see what occurs. I believe the reason you will have the experience is in part because of the information I am giving you today, to help you to see that it couldn't have happened before now, that you have not done anything wrong. It is not that you haven't been diligent enough or anything like that. Part of what is going on with the Venus transit right now, and that is partly why Samarah came now and not before, is that this infusion of the planetary frequency of Venus is really in a sense about a concentration of love. And in that way, doubt and fear can be set aside for a time and you can see things most clearly in this light. If you look through any newspaper or media, you will notice that no one can hide from their errors anymore, from their greed or from the various things they have tried to manipulate. What happened in the past that led others to silence you will not happen now, it is not the same dynamic anymore. There's simply no place to hide. Everything is being revealed. In a sense, everything is being turned over. Just like when you go to plant a new garden and there is stubble from the past, you must turn over the soil so you will have a fresh place in which to grow. This time of 2004 is really about looking at the past clearly and then saying, 'Yes, but now it's a different time. And even if it didn't work two years ago or four years ago or six years ago, it just might work now because I am different and the world is different, quite different.' The truth must be revealed now, and the truth is that the world is yours to create as you choose. There is no one else to do it. Your life, and the lives of so many others, are all about clearing away the debris and writing a new story, one that is about equality and the idea that when you harm someone, you also harm yourself and to understanding that dynamic on every level, from the simple thought that I can touch you with love and that touches others with love, to realize that every part of the universe is infused with your thoughts. As you love, as you create, as you choose true equality and freedom, every corner of the world will begin to have that and will begin to experience that. In this process, abusive powers will fall away and that does creates some chaos right now, absolutely.

"What you have been seeking is where do I fit in all of this strangeness? Well, I will tell you a few things. First of all, your clarity is the most important thing that you can give to yourself. Even when you don't feel clear, you can say, 'I am clear that I don't feel clear.' It is perfect, you see, because that is the truth of your experience in that moment and that begins like a laser to push away everything that is in the way of you seeing clearly. Your mind is like a laser. You have a very bright mind. You can start to say, 'How can I express this love I feel for everyone? What can I do with that?' and now your world will open up in so many possibilities. No one is inherently better than another. It is only better if it feels more liberating, more fulfilling for you.

"You are quite a good writer, you can write. If you do not want to do that, you can speak. If you do not want to do that, you can simply sit in your living room and send love. All of these have a powerful impact because like any light, when it is concentrated it casts a long beam into the darkness.

"What I would say to you is that there is no need for you to wait to have any one way revealed to you that is better than another. When you just allow and say, 'I would just like there to be more love in the world . . . oh, I'm in charge of that? Oh, dear,' (Laughter) and see, here is the shift for so many from, 'I'm in charge of that? But I'm not the president or the head of this. . .' But truly, you are in charge of that, just as everyone is. You can literally sit in your living room and say, 'All right, today I would like to send my love and sense of equality to. . .' and then you fill in the blanks.

"Whatever is in your heart that moment or that day, whether it is the children of the world or animals of the world or air pollution does not matter because what you are doing is taking this brilliant bright light of yours and sending it where there is still darkness. Just as dropping a pebble in a pond creates ripples you can see, this creates changes you will see. It's challenging sometimes because you are sitting there thinking, what good is this really doing? But it is. And I think a part of you knows that it is because you have spent so many lives in prayer, this you know. You know that prayer is like putting a beautiful ball of love out there for anyone who chooses to catch it. You do not always know who catches it but still you know that you put it out there.

"And so that is one way. Your writing and speaking are really up to you, when you are ready. That might never be and that is all right. I don't want you to feel that the world would have been neglected. Now, will the world be richer for it? Yes, I would say yes. But for you to feel that freedom is very important. To write or not to write. To speak or not to speak. I believe that what you can write about is the feeling, the responsibility and the price of freedom, done in such a way that it would not sound like a political speech but like a mother's love. That is what we need to balance the speeches that we are hearing now in the world, because there is a hunger for freedom. There is a hunger for equality and yet there is not an understanding of what must we do to really create it. The means to create the freedom lies within all of you. Not any one person has the answer, has the protocol. 'Here, do this!' Because your world has grown up with people giving you protocols, telling you, 'Here's what to do. Follow these directions. Take two and call me in the morning,' there is a sense of waiting for someone to give you the protocol. Part of the struggle the politicians are having is that so far there is no protocol that is working. Everyone wants the Iraqis to be free. Well, if you have not been free in a generation and right now being free means you can't walk in the street without your children being shot and you can't get a job and you don't have food or water it doesn't make freedom very nice.

"There is still a lot of work to be done. Your job is really to speak what is in your heart, either in writing, through your prayers or through your speech, because you carry that torch. It has been yours for a long, long time. Along with others, for you are not the only one, of course. I believe that what you waited for was, 'But where's the gang? Where's the group? Where's the meeting? Where's the parade?' (Laughter) And you're early in the game so far. I believe there will be many who come out and like blinking their eyes out of the cave will come to see and meet with you. When there is change people are not sure what to do and that is all right. You can sit in your living room and say, 'I'm not sure what to do so today I will pray. I'll pray to be clear and I'll pray to send love and I'll pray to know the next step I will take,' and then it will come. There is no one who will tell you what to do in a way that is meaningful for you. It must be your own signal."

"Can you tell me some of the other lifetimes I have had with you? I feel I was with you during the lifetime of Jesus."

"Well, first of all we were friends, yes. In that life you were also a woman. In that life we had many good times together. We liked to make bread. We liked to walk and we liked to talk. We liked the simple part of that life. You were not Mary Magdalene or one of the other disciples but you were very important in the way that you cared for those who came. You were what you would sort of call a greeter, because we had so many people who came to be with us. You would welcome them and gather them around and tell them where to sit and where to find food. You were always quiet. It was almost like you liked to breath in the love."

"I've always felt a great connection to you. It's my wanting to feel it and remember it."

"A part of that is because you have had lives of not being in a body as well as lives of being in a body. This time, this life, is really about having the joy of being in your body, married to the joy of your love and your spirit. That is why I think going to Lourdes would be very lovely for you. I cannot imagine you would go and not feel again in that place. (Long pause) I am going to tell you something. I was not going to because I hate to cloud your mind."

"Please tell me."

"You were Bernadette."

(Long pause) "Really? That's a complete surprise."

"I know."

"What do I say after that?"

"And that is what you are looking for again."

"What do I say?"

"You do not have to say anything, darling. You just have to remember. Just take a moment."

"Oh, thank you for sharing that with me. It's going to take a few minutes for me to get past this."

"You do not have to get past it. It is not to get past. You have wanted to feel it. Take a moment. Let your mind be all right, because now you will remember. Now you will remember."

(At this point the session was stopped while we hugged and I cried and then tried to regain my composure.)

"Please tell me as much as you can about that lifetime until I can remember it."

"Well, yes. But right now it is your body remembering, trust that. Trust your own remembering. Your mind wants all the details but it is your body shivering with remembrance. This is what you have been waiting for. To feel the truth. When you were Bernadette, you tried to tell everyone and no one wanted to believe you. That was what was so hard for you, so hard for you that in this life you created that doubting Thomas within yourself."

"This is astounding. I never expected this. Of course everybody thinks they're special in the eyes of God, but I never expected this. What a treasure. What a gift you have given me, again."

"In that life you had your innocence which is why I came. There was still all that political stuff going on. They would say, 'Oh, she's just a girl. She can't even read. Why would Mary come and see her?' and you knew I came because of your love. And again, it was all about equality. That is why I come to everyone, so of course I would come to you. Of course I would come. You had the ears to listen and the eyes to see and the heart to believe."

"You've been with me always?"

"Always, you can't get rid of me. (Laughter) Now we have broken through again."

"I feel a euphoria!"

"Yes, because everything is together. Your mind and your heart and your body are all together because now you know."

"Now I know. All this time and now I know."

"Yes and your body knows. You decide whom you will tell, it is up to you. It is certainly not a secret, but you know what I mean."

"Yes, I know."

"You can share it if you wish but you know how it can be misunderstood."

"But I can share it with a few people?"

"Certainly."

"Oh, thank you, thank you. Do you come in my dreams?"

"First of all, you do not need a hall pass to come see me. All right?

"I get that now."

"All that was in the way is gone. And so we are just like old friends. We will walk in the garden again. We will be out in the night sky."

"This is what I've been wanting forever. It's too good to be true."

"Oh no, don't say that. It is so good it must be true. It is so good it must be true."

"Thank you."

"I can see you dancing in the garden again. From now on, wherever you are, we can just have a conversation like we are having now. You will know me. So like I said, do not speak to a lot of people because like you, some of them are still wanting and wanting and they will want it from you somehow. Just allow it to be the experience we share."

"When the time is right will you help me share this with the world?"

"Yes, it is all going to be easy now. The veil is lifted. Yes, you did it." (Laughter)

"Oh Mary, thank you."

"You look like a little girl again, just like I remember."

"Can I ask more questions about that lifetime?"

"Certainly, yes."

"My brothers and sisters in that lifetime, are any of them in my life now?"

"Yes, some of them are."

"Can you share that?"

"Let's not go there right now."

"Okay. This is enough for a lifetime."

"What I want you to stay with right now is the feeling of knowing. From this everything else vibrates and comes to you."

"How can I forget this feeling?"

"You won't, you won't, but I mean just to let yourself have it. Let yourself have it."

"Now I see why you wanted me to go to Lourdes. I'm going to have to get there. If I feel like this here, imagine how I would feel there. There's so much I want to share with you."

"What I would like you to do from now on is, when you feel like it, to keep a separate journal, *My Walk With Mary*. You can start with your life as Bernadette."

"Will I remember more?"

"Yes, but I do not want to tell you. I want you to just say, 'I was a little girl in the south of France,' and see what happens."

"Maybe it would help if I got more books on Bernadette?"

"You can if you like, but I want you to trust your heart because the story that comes from inside you is the truth."

"At some time you want me to share this with the world?"

"Yes."

"I just knew there was something I was supposed to share."

"It is this story. I am calling it *My Walk With Mary*, but you can call it whatever you like."

"You said don't share it right now?"

"Not this moment, because I want you to develop confidence in what you are writing."

"Thank you, thank you."

"No, thank you."

"You're thanking me?"

"Yes, because without you, how does my story come to others?"

"This is just too powerful for this little person to take in."

"No, it is not. You are not a little person. You are a child of God and a beautiful daughter."

"Sometimes I feel I'm not doing the right thing."

"I have no complaints. This human life is not always easy."

"What do I do now?"

"Just feel. You see, when you feel, from that everything comes, everything comes. You do not have to worry because when you are integrated and radiating the way that you are, everything just naturally occurs."

"So this is the purpose of my lifetime? To bring this message of Mary to the world?"

"It is to talk about how love and faith transformed your life. People want to hear one person's story that they might feel their own."

"I understand."

"So, it is about your walk with me. That will help so many people."

"So before I incarnated I had agreed to become Bernadette?"

"Well, yes. We had to do something after your time in the Middle Ages. (Laughter) You see, it is because you have always worked with equality and faith and love."

"Oh, I feel so special."

"You are, you are."

"I've always felt special but everyone's special in the eyes of God."

"Yes, that is true, but as each of you discovers your gift it is like that first Christmas morning when you say, 'This is mine?'"

"This is mine?"

"And this is yours."

"Thank you for sharing it with me. You wanted me to find out myself but…"

"I did, but then I sat with the energy and felt you could take it today and also that it is going to help you right now. You were ready for it right now."

"I feel a great connection with Jesus and St. Germain."

"It is because you allow it and also because in this life you are what you call an old soul and you have been around long enough to have those folks as friends. Now that you know all this information, it is also to talk about this life and your walk with me in this life."

"My life is answered. All my waiting is over."

"Yes, your waiting is over. So today go and celebrate in whatever way you choose. Eat and drink and say, 'my waiting is over.'"

"You'll help me with the book?"

"Yes, every step of the way. So we will end for the moment even though I am not leaving. I am just allowing this beautiful energy of your knowing to penetrate every cell of your being in your body. Know that you are my beautiful, beautiful daughter and that all is well. You are well and you are loved."

Chapter III

Many of you know the story of Bernadette and the apparitions at Lourdes. You may have been taught about it in religion class or perhaps watched her life story on television. Some reading this may never have heard of Bernadette at all.

Either way, I would like to give you a brief history of her life. The version I am about to present to you is the one the world is familiar with, but as you will see, the real reason Mary came to Bernadette and gave to her a very important message has never been revealed until now.

Bernarde Marie was born in Boily, France on Sunday, January 7, 1844 to Louise and Francois Soubirous. She was baptized on January 9th and her name was changed to Marie Bernarde. Because of her tiny build, her family nicknamed her Bernadette.

The Soubirous had nine children though only five survived. Bernadette was the oldest child. Marie, also known as Antoinette, was born in 1846, Jean Marie in 1851, Justin in 1855, and Pierre in 1859.

When Bernadette was ten months old, her mother was severely burned and was unable to continue breastfeeding. Louise had a friend in Bartres who had just lost a son in childbirth and she agreed to be a wet nurse for Bernadette.

At twenty-six months, the age of weaning, Bernadette returned home to her family at the mill. When Bernadette was ten years old, her father lost his position at the mill and the family was forced to leave their home.

In 1855 cholera broke out in Lourdes. Bernadette was affected by the plague, which left her weak and asthmatic. It was a combination of asthma and tuberculosis of the bones in her legs that ultimately led her to her death at the young age of thirty-five.

In 1856 Bernadette's father was working as a day laborer while her mother took in laundry. As a result, Bernadette was put in charge of her siblings and was unable to attend school or go to Catechism classes. Now living in extreme poverty, Francois moved his family to the Cachot (dungeon), a damp and unhealthy room that had previously been used as a prison.

In 1857 Bernadette returned to the home of her wet nurse in Bartres. Her assistance was needed there as a babysitter and a maid. Her duties also included tending to the sheep and pigs. At this time, Bernadette was trying to learn her catechism in order to prepare for her Holy Communion. Because of her duties and her limited learning abilities Bernadette found this very difficult.

In January of 1858, Bernadette's homesickness got the better of her and she returned home to the love of her family, still living in poverty at the "dungeon." On the morning of February 11th,

Bernadette, her sister Antoinette and their friend, Jeanne Abadie went to the area of Massabielle to collect bundles of firewood and bones to sell. Before crossing the canal to go to the other side where her sister and her friend already were, Bernadette heard a loud noise amidst the shrubbery above the Massabielle grotto. She looked over and noticed that the shrubbery was shaking and that there was something white behind it that looked to be a girl. Bernadette gazed at the apparition, then fell to her knees and began to pray. The apparition smiled at her and moved into the grotto.

This was the first of eighteen visitations to Bernadette by the Blessed Mother. During the seventeen subsequent visits, it is reported that Mother Mary spoke to Bernadette. She asked if Bernadette would return for fifteen days and requested that Bernadette pray for the conversion of sinners. Mary also told Bernadette that she could not promise her happiness in this world but only in the next. Mary also told Bernadette to instruct the priests to build a chapel on the site and to drink at the fountain and wash herself there.

Not seeing a fountain, Bernadette headed toward the river. She was told that was not the place and Mary indicated with her finger to go to the bottom of the grotto. Obeying, Bernadette went there and found only a little slimy water. The water was so dirty that after three attempts Bernadette had to throw the water away. On the fourth try, she was able to drink from it.

She was also asked to eat of an herb found there. Along with the request for a chapel to be built, Bernadette was also asked by the Blessed Mother to go and tell the priests to come here in procession.

The last words spoken to Bernadette by the apparition were, "I am the Immaculate Conception."

Bernadette's life was not an easy one, both during and after the apparitions. She was grilled relentlessly by both town officials and the Church. Even when she entered the convent in July of 1866, she met with resistance and jealousy from nuns at the motherhouse in Nevers. In 1867 Bernadette renewed her vows. In religious life she kept her baptismal name. She was now Sister Marie Bernarde.

Due to her ill health, she was given the task of working in the convent's infirmary and helping in the kitchen. During her time in Nevers she was given the Sacrament of Extreme Unction at least four times.

On April 16, 1879 Sister Marie Bernarde died from complications of asthma and tuberculosis of the bones. She was thirty-five. Her body lies in state at the Saint Gilard Convent of the Sisters of Charity of Nevers, incorrupt to this day.

Chapter IV

When the channeling was over, Samarah suggested that I take a few minutes somewhere quiet to try and let what had just occurred settle in.

Tears were streaming down my face, tears of joy, excitement, release and simply tears of the love I had just felt in that room. I knew without a doubt that I had been in the presence of Mother Mary. I have never had an experience so profound. I felt like I was home.

I remained in the bookstore for a while because I knew I would not be able to drive. How I got home safely was a miracle. My angels must have been paying attention because I certainly was not. I was in shock. My mind was spinning. What just happened? I kept repeating Mother Mary's words over and over. I was experiencing a feeling in my body that I had never felt, a feeling in my chest area of not just a tingling sensation but more of an expansion, like it was about to burst! I was euphoric. I also felt validated for all those feelings I'd had all my life about something I just couldn't put my finger on, something so huge that it would change the direction of my life. Until today it always seemed just out of my reach. Well, now I can say that I not only found it but I'm grabbing it with both hands.

I couldn't wait to go home and tell my friend. I knew that until I said it out loud it would all seem too surreal. Mother Mary suggested that I not tell a lot of people and I already had in mind the handful of friends I would tell.

My housemate was used to me by now. She knew all the classes and workshops I've taken and she has seen all the metaphysical books I bring home, but I don't think she was ready for this. I prepared her as best I could, but how do you tell someone that you were just told you are the reincarnation of Saint Bernadette? I think she took it very well. I was pacing back and forth the entire time; my mind and body were on overdrive. It was as though something inside me had just awakened from a deep sleep. I was too excited to sit. I suggested we call another dear friend of ours and arrange to meet for dinner. Knowing that nothing in life happens accidentally, it will be of no surprise to learn that this friend had been to Lourdes a few years before. She had gone as a malade with the Knights of Malta. In French, malade means a sick or ill person. Once a year the Knights of Malta lead a pilgrimage to Lourdes bringing several malades. My friend was recovering from major back surgery at the time and had been sponsored for the trip.

When we met for dinner, I told her of my incredible day. She immediately said that I should go to Lourdes with the Knights of Malta. Their next pilgrimage was at the end of April 2005. My mind was racing at this point.

The Knights of Malta, as I was soon to find out, is filled with wonderful and loving people. The Order of Malta is a lay, religious, pontifical order of the Catholic Church. It is governed by a Grand Master who bears the rank of Cardinal and reports directly to His Holiness, the Pope. The purpose of the Order is to promote the spiritual well being of its members by encouraging them to dedicate themselves personally to the sick and to the poor, as well as to defend the Faith as members of a religious community. In addition to accomplishing these objectives, the Order is also the oldest established charitable institution in the world, running hospitals and ambulance corps in many countries, establishing mission hospitals, providing disaster relief, and administering to the poor around the world. The combination of all the good works and spiritual outpourings of the Order are epitomized by their annual pilgrimage to Lourdes. The American Association, together with Knights, Dames and Auxiliaries from all over the world, join together each spring to care for the sick, the handicapped and their care givers on this pilgrimage to Our Lady of Lourdes. When my friend mentioned going with them as an Auxiliary, I couldn't think of a better way to start my own personal pilgrimage.

As Mother Mary suggested, I went home that night and started a journal I called, *My Walk With Mary*. Could I have called it anything else? From time-to-time I will be referring to the journal, but I would like to write word for word what I wrote that night.

> June 9, 2004 Nothing could have prepared me for what I heard today. Although deep in my heart there was always a stirring, I had no idea of the enormity of the truth. Today I found out among

other intertwined lives that I am the reincarnation of Saint Bernadette of Lourdes. It was suggested by Mother Mary, through her channel, Samarah, that I start this journal. Mother Mary told me that the lifetime as Bernadette would reveal itself to me and now is the time. I am writing in faith that I will be guided. The reality of it all is too overwhelming right now for me to comprehend but I know somewhere deep in my soul it is true.

For the next few days and weeks it was very difficult for me to focus on anything other than what had just occurred. I was functioning day to day but just barely. I wasn't sleeping at all. I'd hear the clock ticking out the hours while I lay in bed tossing and turning. It was all I could think about. How could this amazing reality be happening to me? But it was. It was all true and I knew it. I also knew that this was a very special gift and I had to treat it that way.

As the weeks and months went by, I was gradually making plans to go to Lourdes. My friend was contacting the people she had become very close to as the result of her trip. Thinking positively, I obtained a passport. I wanted to be ready.

I continued writing in my journal as Mother Mary asked, knowing that this personal information could one day be shared with many people. I wrote about my love for Our Lady and how grateful and honored I felt. I also wrote about the fear I had about living up to expectations. What if I couldn't remember? What if I travel all the way to France and nothing happens? What will other people think when they find out this incredible story? And yet none of my fears were going to stop me from going. I knew in my soul that this was my destiny.

Growing up Catholic, I knew the story of Bernadette, the young girl who saw and spoke with the Blessed Mother. I always envied her. Imagine, I thought, what that must have been like, to actually see Our Lady, to be in her presence, to be the one she chose to appear to. Little did I realize as a young girl myself the events that would unfold in my own life. I have always felt a strong bond with Mary. I always thought it was because I was named after her, but now I understand why my feelings went so deep.

I longed to speak to her again. I felt her presence near me always, but I ached for another "meeting." Then I found out that Samarah was returning in October. My wish was granted.

Chapter V

My next visit with Samarah was on Saturday, October 16, 2004. I was counting down the days with great anticipation. It had been four months since our last meeting, and there was so much for us to share.

As soon as I walked into the room where the channeling was to take place, I felt a great sense of peace. Samarah greeted me and we proceeded to catch up on what was happening in our lives. She knew that I was planning to go to Lourdes with the Knights of Malta. She told me that the Island of Malta was a place where the Divine Feminine and Goddess cultures had thrived for thousands of years and that traces of the Goddess culture still exist there. She explained that when she said Goddess culture, she meant that it wasn't patriarchal. She said that it is the kind of society we are trying to build today, not power over but power with. She also said that for the last year or so she had been thinking of going to Malta. She felt that it was time to seed this beautiful energy she carried and found it very interesting that I was going to Lourdes with the Knights of Malta.

As we settled in, Samarah started the session in her usual way, by asking that we be surrounded by the Holy Light of Father/Mother God, that the angels, guides and teachers who work with us draw near and that the over lighting angels that are here at all times spread their wings of courage, compassion, loyalty and love. She welcomed and invoked all the archangels Michael, Gabriel, Uriel and Rafael. She thanked them for joining us and sharing their generosity, wisdom and love. She then invited and evoked the presence of Mother Mary, asking that she be a clear channel for her information and that all that was spoken be of the highest good for the receiver, herself and for all beings everywhere.

The following is a full recounting of that session. Mother Mary speaks first.

"Hello darling, how are you?"

"I'm fine, thank you."

"I see you with your suitcases. Is it time yet?" (Laughter)

"I know, I can't wait to go."

"And to be so excited to go. I'm so grateful and glad."

"I'm just so excited. I can't wait."

"As we spoke the last time, to go to such a place is always filled with mystery and wonder and beauty. And in a way to go with all those you are going with will make it even more of a memorable trip for you. I would like you to buy a little journal specifically for this trip although you can begin now to write about how this trip has come about for you. And it is going to be if you choose a lovely book to share. You can call it anything you like, but the feeling is in the footsteps of Bernadette. Do you feel that?"

"Yes, I do."

"Remember that a journal is a personal revealing of oneself. And so whatever you choose, from your greatest excitement to anything else that arrives, fear, doubt, whatever, know that in your writing are all the emotions felt not only by you but by all others who have this journey in mind. You can imagine all those you push in the wheelchairs, with their hopes and their fears. And to whatever extent you choose, you can also write their stories, with their permission, of course. Let them know you want to write a true accounting of the journey in the footsteps of Bernadette. There will be some stories that will bring you to tears and will allow this book to be, I want to say, the truth of this journey, because so many go with their stories untold. Thousands and thousands have come to Lourdes. Millions maybe, I don't know, and each of them has a story. And all of those who think of going and don't go, they also have a story.

"If you are to write your journey, beginning with what occurred in our first encounter, it would be so rich for so many, for those who go and those who would like to go. It is as if you can take them by the hand and show them a journey that was true for you and in that process teach them a little about faith and fear and hope and miracles."

"I'd love to be able to write that book."

"You will, and don't worry at all, please. As you sit with your journal and write, you will have it ninety percent perfect and later, a little polishing here and there. When you sit and write, it comes from your heart and from the truth of you. Please don't worry about the spelling and grammar, don't even think about that. One of the most powerful books was one written by Anne Frank and no one worried that she may have misspelled a word or that the grammar was backwards here or there, it does not matter. So please, don't even let that come into your field of thought. Just say, 'All right, I am going to write my story of this journey and how it began.' Between now and the time you go, you may not pick the book up everyday. There will be days when you write and days when you don't, but already the story has begun."

"I've already started."

"Yes, and you can see that it is already becoming a beautiful journey in the footsteps of Bernadette."

"When I go to Lourdes and have my experience and write that I was Bernadette, there will be some people who won't believe me."

"Some will and some won't. It will be beyond some people's understanding at this moment. And that's all right. You will simply be sharing what is true for you. People have come to Samarah and have said, 'How do you know it's Mother Mary? Show me your proof.' Here is a funny story. A priest in Santa Fe wrote to Samarah by e-mail and said, 'I wish to tell you you're not channeling Mother Mary and you really should stop. Mother Mary would never say as you do on your web site to talk to Buddha and to say that Buddha had any life whatsoever. She would only talk about Jesus.' And you know, Samarah just smiled and wrote back in a beautiful way, saying, 'You know, I really appreciate you taking the time to write me and you have such an honoring practice of Mother Mary. I really appreciate that, and I have my experience of Mother Mary and I really hope you can honor that. The Mother Mary I know would not shut the door on anyone, atheist, Buddhist or anyone. That's the Mother Mary I know. But I honor you and the Mother Mary you know.' And he never wrote back again. It was probably some food for thought.

"So you see, you may have some people say, 'Well, how do you know that you had this life?' And you can say, 'You know, this is my experience and it's my knowledge and these were the visions, memories and feelings I had and if it's not true for you, then that's all right. I don't have to prove anything. I'm simply sharing my experience.' I think more and more people, hopefully, will begin to trust in their own experience instead of a mental belief system that has nothing to do with the truth of their being that loaded into them almost like a computer program. The important thing to recognize is that any program is there to be useful to a certain extent. But the highest use of any human being is to know you have your own experience, which no one can take away from you, based on the true, what I call, revelation of love. And when you felt that revelation of love, no one could take it away from you."

"I still have it right here in my heart."

"Absolutely. And that is what guides you now and what will create this beautiful book and your experiences. Be open. Go and say, 'I'm here.' The beauty is that once you have that, those who hunger to know their own revelation will gather around you because in your truth, they can find truth of their own. The old teaching, 'Know ye the truth and the truth shall set you free,' that is what you now know. And it is hard because you can't always just give that to someone. It is a revelation, meaning it is revealed to them. But the joy that you will have from now on is simply the joy of sharing your revelation, not because it's theirs but because in the truth of yours comes the peeling away, if they choose, of course, of these old programs that said, 'Oh, God only comes to this one or that one,' because of the story of Bernadette. And in your book, we see a few pages in the introduction that summarizes the story of Bernadette and then throughout a weaving back into your own experiences as well. Once Bernadette had spoken with me, no one could tell her she hadn't because she knew."

"Just like I knew."

"Exactly. Archangel Michael is known to have the sword of truth and the shield of light. He is often depicted with a sword and with a shield and people wonder why he is seen as a warrior? You'll discover more of that and about Michael in your journey as well. The sword is merely to cut through illusion. It's not to hurt anyone, but to cut through the veils of illusion. The shield is to show that we all carry the ability to have a field so strong in light that no one's doubts can penetrate it. That is what you have now. No one's doubt can affect your knowing. Sometimes you will feel it and sometimes you will hear it. You will hold their hand and say, 'I too in the past had moments of doubt, but I now know for myself the truth that has set me free!'"

"I still don't have the memory, but I have the feeling."

"The memories will come. You know, in some ways, it's like wanting an experience so much that you are concentrating too much to actually experiences it. It's like any magical rainbow. If you're watching on a rainy day saying, 'I want a rainbow. I want a rainbow. I want a rainbow!' It's not the same as if you say, 'Oh look, a rainbow!' but that's really how it will come to you. So I would tell you to just put that aside and concentrate on the few months left before you leave to get your arrangements in order, to get your journal, whatever. You can do a little research, if you'd like, about these Knights of Malta. The Knights of Malta believe in the Divine Feminine, that's the simplest way to explain it. There could be a weaving of that into your story as well. Let it be very casual."

"I'd like to ask a little more about Lourdes. What was your purpose in coming to Bernadette? People go there for physical and spiritual healing. Was that your purpose? Why is it that some people receive a healing and others don't?"

"My purpose in coming to Lourdes was to break the hold that the priests held over the people."

"At that time?"

"Still, still. My purpose for coming then and continuing at Lourdes is to try and teach anyone and everyone that one does not need a priest to know God. That some benefit from that process is marvelous, but what I am working so hard to do is to create a direct experience of God, Spirit and Mary for any and all who are open to that thought. Because, as we said at the beginning, when you know, your life becomes a radiant process. And that is what I wish for all of you.

"The difficulty, and you will see it when you get there, is that the Catholic Church perches right atop the Grotto. And though the Catholic Church continues to do good things, they hold the reigns of power as if they are the ones who knew me. Herein is the irony. I came to Bernadette, not to the priests, but they want to hold the authority and power. Part of what you are doing and what so many are doing today is not spending energy railing against the Church. To fight any war is to perpetuate it. Better instead to say, 'I have had a direct experience.' That is truly what everyone is wishing for, to have one's own direct experience. That is why they go.

"The water at Lourdes continues to have the purity and the grace of unconditional love and it continues to flow in order to offer that to everyone. Why, you ask, do some experience healing and some not? The simplest explanation is that when you come to this world, you come with a contract, a sacred contract and the purpose of your life here is to remember that contract and fulfill it. Now, if you come to Lourdes avoiding the truth of your life, you will probably not receive healing because you are still going through whatever you are going through, and to have that illuminated that you must remember and move on. To take back the Divine Power, that is the purpose. Those that experience healing are ready for that grace, are ready for that change, and are ready for that opening. Do I wish that everyone could be healed? Absolutely. Absolutely, but it is not yet the time for that."

"You can't be involved because of our free will?"

"It is offered, but they must claim it. Now, let us give an example of that in your own life. After our last meeting, you could have gone home and said, 'Samarah doesn't know what she's doing. I don't believe that for a minute. I'm going to go back to my life and do this or that.' You could have done that and your life would have been different than it is right now. Opportunities come into every life. Again and again we come and say, 'Hello, we're here. We love you.

You are amazing and radiant and powerful.' And when someone finally says, 'Oh, all right, yes.' there is truly a celebration for you and for all of us. 'Oh yes, she's got it!' (Hands clapping)

"Now you are really moving into even more of your sacred contract, which is to help people experience their own power, their own Divine love. Just as I can't make them do this, neither can you. But by offering your story, your true story, others think to themselves, 'Oh my, she's an ordinary girl and look what happened to her. Perhaps something could also happen to me.' That is why the Bernadette energy is what you carry, that of an ordinary girl. Of course there is no such thing, but that is how people will view it. You know that you were not a saint, you were not this or that, and you were not a priest." (Laughter)

"So this is my soul contract? This is why I've come, to share this story?"

"Yes."

"I knew there was something I was supposed to share. I've been searching for so long. I just could never put my finger on it. But now to know and be directed towards it, it's just wonderful."

"Yes, it simplifies everything, it really does. And I think some of the people that will come to you, of all different kinds, from those who are suffering from physical disabilities, to emotional distress, in a way they would like you to fix them. Now, here is the part that gets a little challenging. Neither you nor I can heal or fix anyone, as much as we would love to. But what we can do is to offer them bountiful amounts of love and light, knowledge and possibilities. And when you do that, you are being a healer and you are being a teacher. After that, it is for them to choose to keep the old programming of, 'You're not worth anything, you're stupid, you're this or that,' or to let that hard drive crash. Will they allow a revelation to come through them and to them? Those like you who have had revelations carry a beautiful responsibility to share it, and that is all."

"That's been my dream, to share it. I just never knew how. I became a massage therapist, a Reiki Master, a hypnotherapist, but now I see. It's going to be through this book. My life is going to change after this book comes out. Can you tell me a little about that?"

"Yes, I can tell you a few things. First I would like to go back to Samarah. You have so much in common. You know, when I first came, she was worried that there would be people in lawn chairs camped out in her yard saying the Rosary, waiting for her to come out and do magical hocus-pocus. And she said, 'Oh Mary, I just couldn't stand that.' And so I said to her, 'Then darling, don't create it, don't choose it.' As you take this time before your journey and as you are writing just decide, 'All right, I am to be an author and to share this book. How do I want that to look?' There are authors like Wayne Dyer, he loves to go out and have many groups and travel. He certainly doesn't have to do it anymore for financial reasons, but he loves to do it. It's his passion to tell his story and share his knowledge. Others are much quieter in the way they share their knowing. For a long time after Shirley MacLaine wrote her first few books she did tours and things but now you barely hear what she is doing. It really will be under your control what level of visibility you decide to have. The book will take its own course. It will easily find a publisher. It will easily find its way out there. And you will find, as I said, that there will be some who say, 'Oh, poppycock!' but that's all right. In terms of your travels and your journeys, many will hunger, just as Samarah, to have you right in the room to tell your story because reading the book evoked their curiosity and their interest. But to see you, to feel you, to hear you share, that's heaven for them. So what I would say, especially for the first year or two when the book is out, to whatever extent you feel you would like to get out there, it would be very much appreciated, very much."

"Did you have something to do with my mother calling me Mary? I had an aunt named Mary, but my mother said, 'No, I named you after the Blessed Mother.'"

"Well, yes. Yes, you know some mothers are wise enough to know the energies of their children. When Samarah's son was born he was to be called John after his father, but Samarah looked at him and he looked at her and she said, 'Oh, you're Michael,' and so he is Michael. Some mothers are wise enough to know that."

"About twenty years ago, another channel told me that I would be speaking in front of a lot of people. She said it was like the picture of the Hermit in the Tarot cards. He turns around and sheds light onto them with his lantern and they all say, 'Yes, that's it. This is what I've been waiting for.' Is this it?"

"Yes, this is it. Isn't it exciting?"

"Wow, I've been waiting for so long."

"Yes you have, but what I want to tell you is that your journey to be a massage therapist, a Reiki Master, a hypnotherapist, that was what partly cleared away the old programming, the old ideas and the old thoughts. I'm just using the concept, you crashed that hard drive in those experiences. They were absolutely essential to put you in a place where you could hear and feel what you now hear and feel. For many it's not something where you can say, 'Oh yes, just sit over there and you'll get your revelation.' It's to share all of your journey. It didn't happen when you were two or five or eight years old, it happened at this point in your life when you could really savor it and trust it. That is another part of your sharing that will help so many. How do you trust these experiences? How do you allow that experience and not say, 'Oh, I must be crazy because I had a vision or I heard voices or something like that.' People do have those moments, and they say to themselves, 'Oh, that's crazy. It couldn't be that.' You will also be sharing with them about what I call "soul sight," being able to see not only the human things of what is in front of them, but also from the vision of the soul. And it is a powerful, powerful shift to take back a person's power and authority and knowing so they do not need a priest in order to feel God. They will know that it's right here, all of the time. And that will lead them on their path of grace as you share your story."

"I've waited my whole life for this. When I came on my first session and you recognized my energy did you say, 'Yeah, here she is, it's time. She's finally ready?'"

"Yes. You know, waiting is not quite like that. It's more like when a child is born and they're just three months old. Are you waiting for them to take their first step? A part of you is, but another part doesn't want them to take their first step at three months old because they could hurt themselves. Do you see what I mean? So yes, I was very, very happy to see you and yes, I knew it was time, but it could not have happened before then. Do you know what I mean? So it was a joyful, 'Yeah, here she is.'"

"Sometimes I get a ringing in my ears. Is that a confirmation from you? I know you are with me all the time, but how will I know you're here? Sometimes I really miss you."

"Some of it will be when you share your life and your story. Because for instance, right now, where is Samarah? She's dwelling in this field of grace. So there is no more really missing me. You are me and you are Bernadette and you are also the lady Mary that walks in this life. It's like you're fully entering a field that's always been there but has been a little remote due to focusing on other things. And so I don't think you'll miss me. You'll just merge with me because you have become all of the "Mary-ness" that you are."

"I know that we and Mother Earth are getting close to our ascension. Can you tell me a little bit about that? Can you tell me if this is my last incarnation on Earth?"

"All right, we have to put aside some of that thought for a moment. The fifth dimension is right here, right now, you and me, because here we are Samarah, Mary, Mother Mary, Bernadette, all of that. What is ascension? It is allowing oneself to be ascended. It is not to go anywhere. It is to bring that fullness of all of you right here, right now. So, you are already in the fifth dimension right now because you can experience it when you can put your hands on your heart and say, 'Oh, yes.' It's as though, instead of taking an elevator up, you become the elevator. You are available in every way. If someone knocked on the door, you could turn around and open it but meanwhile you can hear the angels sing. This is ascension. You become your multi-dimensional self. It's more like, 'Where is my focus in the moment?' If you are driving you have to focus on driving, but if you pull over for a while you could easily and immediately allow yourself to see things from a different perspective. It's as if you've opened up to the elevator, to use a common image. You are allowing yourself to be, at any moment, the appropriate frequency for that moment. And so it's not really that you are going anywhere, but that you are bringing the dimensionality that is available to everyone here."

"The Kingdom of God is within."

"It is within and it is becoming here. Samarah's book, I believe, is going to be called *Amazing Grace*. And that is really another answer to your question. 'It was grace that taught my heart.' So here you are, in this grace. And when you have this grace, you do still bring it to opening the door and driving the car. And so, in a funny way, I would say, Mary, that you have already ascended because you can now go, it's not really up and down, but it's the easiest way to describe it, and you can be where you need to be but still with all of you. When you take someone's wheelchair, it is a physical act. Yes, you are with them, but also all of you is with them so they are feeling, if they allow it, as though an angel is pushing them."

"I also have a question about my health. I have a brother and two sisters and three out of four of us have had trouble with our eyes. The three of us all had detached retinas. I am actually blind in my left eye. Is this something that we brought forward with us from a past life, or is it something we wanted to experience for some reason in this lifetime?"

"Well, it's a combination. In the past, each of you was blind in several of your lives and in those lives you learned to hear and feel more strongly because you could not rely on your sight. It heightened your other senses, and in this life to some extent you are still compensating by heightening your other senses. What I would like to suggest for you and the others, if they are listening and are ready for it, is that beautiful song, "Amazing Grace." I once was lost, but now I'm found. I once was blind, but now I see. And I see the everyday world and I see the infinite world. And so I ask my eyes to work together and blend together so I can see in every dimension in whatever way is appropriate."

"Do you see me keeping my sight?"

"Let me be clear. It is always a choice Mary, you know that. And to say, 'I choose to see. I choose to see everything, from the pain and suffering all the way to the grace.' It is important to think about seeing through the eyes of grace. So when you see someone suffering, in pain or having some difficulty, you are going to see that, but the way Jesus healed and Mother Theresa healed and others healed is to see through that to the beautiful soul, not focusing on the difficulty they are exhibiting. Focus on the soul, on its being. They will feel that love in their being. And that too is how Christ healed. He didn't see the leper, he saw the angel. And so, as you work with your sight to see everything and have it be all right, your eyes will be fine.

"Part of why you carry this energy is because up until now you have been an ordinary girl. That is so important because people feel this only happens to exalted saints or something and that is not true. Exalt yourselves through the choices that you make. You will continue to attend to the person in the wheelchair, I guess I will use that as an example, but will always be listening for the other world's guidance. The world may say anything, but you know the truth."

"I feel a great connection to Saint Germain."

"Yes, Saint Germain is working very hard to transmute negative energy using the Violet Flame. What does that mean to you or anyone else? What it means is that when someone is experiencing difficulty it is absolutely true and real for them. Absolutely. And there is a way to penetrate the density of that experience by using light. That is really what Saint Germain does. And all of you do that work with Saint Germain through your Reiki, through your thought, through your love and your words. Because all of those actions are designed to penetrate the density that allows that person in difficulty to feel like, 'Well, you don't understand. I'm suffering with…' and you fill in the blank and say, 'I do understand how painful that is, let me just hold you hand.' And now you are sending Reiki or love to them."

"This is Heaven."

"Well, you know darling, this *is* Heaven. This is ascension. And I tell you that because I know you are not going to walk out that door and say, 'Well, I'm this or that.'"

"No. I, like Samarah, feel humbled."

"Yes."

"You're going to help me with my book?"

"Yes."

"*My Walk With Mary*, that's what you want me to call it?"

"Well, you have several books."

"I have several books?"

"Absolutely, because from this trip other things will come. This is the rest of your life. Just keep listening and seeing and trusting and knowing and choosing. That is all you have to do because you have come to this place and said 'Yes.'"

"Thank you."

"And now we will end with a little blessing. I guess there is no such thing as a little blessing. But know, Mary, that you now know the truth for yourself. You have been set free that you might help others still in bondage to realize that they have the key to their own handcuffs, head cuffs (laughter). And it is by sharing your love, your story and your truth, by not trying to fix or heal anyone, but simply being the radiant light of God that you are. Much, much love, darling."

That night this is what I wrote in my journal.

What a wonderful day. I met again with Samarah and Mother Mary and we spoke as old friends. We talked mostly of Lourdes and my book. Mother confirmed that this was my soul contract. I am so blessed. It is all right in front of me now and everything I had always suspected is true. There was something truly special for me to do. She said there would be more than one book. It's hard to express on paper the joy I feel in my heart. Samarah and I also seem to be forming a friendship. I'd like that very much. Thank you.

Chapter VI

Although I already knew in my heart that I would be going to Lourdes with the Knights of Malta, there is a formal process that you need to go through. On January 8, 2005 I met with the couple who were co-chairs of the trip. As I mentioned previously, everyone I had met that was associated with this organization were the most loving and caring people I have ever had the privilege to know, and this couple was no exception. They sponsored my friend who went to Lourdes as a malade. Consequently, I was already acquainted with them. Their love of Our Lady and their dedication to these Pilgrimages was very evident.

They invited me into their home for an interview. I wished to go to Lourdes as an Auxiliary, one who assists the Knights and Dames with the malades and their caregivers. We spoke for a few hours. They were telling me of past Pilgrimages, and I was telling them of my great desire to go.

I wish to tell you now that had I never seen or heard about Samarah or whom she channeled I would certainly still have wanted to go to Lourdes. I have loved the Blessed Mother all my life and to be able to be of service to her in this way would be a real blessing.

At the end of our meeting, I filled out an application and gave them a deposit. I was on my way.

In March I finally told my family that I was going to Lourdes. I mentioned nothing about my connection with Bernadette. They were all very happy and at the same time very surprised. I am not the type of person who does a lot of traveling much less leave the country.

I was starting to get information from the Order of Malta regarding the trip: a list of suggested items to bring, activities that would be taking place, the food that would be served, information about the weather, how much luggage you could bring and also a caregivers handbook. As an Auxiliary, there is a certain "uniform" to be worn throughout the Pilgrimage – a white blouse and skirt, red sweater or blazer, tan nylons and black shoes – so I went shopping.

As the time drew closer, I decided to listen once more to the tapes from the channelings. As I listened, I realized that this trip was not going to be all about me. Yes, I originally wanted to go to Lourdes to see if I would remember my life as Bernadette, but now it had grown to be so much more than that. I was not just going for selfish reasons. I was going on a pilgrimage.

The time had finally came. On the morning of April 27, 2005 I left Boston with a bus full of other pilgrims en route to the Newark, NJ Airport. I knew this was going to be a very long trip. We left Boston a little before noon and arrived in Newark around 4:00 PM. Our flight was delayed and we didn't take off until approximately 10:00 PM. Although I was with a big group going on a chartered flight, I was still a little nervous. This was the first time I was traveling without a close friend. I was very proud of myself. I just followed the group and what I didn't know I just asked.

It was a long flight and I didn't really sleep. I think the combination of excitement and anticipation kept me awake. We arrived at the Lourdes-Tarbes Airport around 4:30 AM, but with the time difference it was 10:30 AM local time. By this time, I had my second wind, which was good because we hit the ground running. We went straight to the hotels and unpacked. Because Lourdes is at the foot of the Pyrenees Mountains, the weather in spring tends to be cold and rainy. We were advised to bring warm clothes such as skiwear, gloves, long underwear and a raincoat, but when we arrived it was sunny, beautiful and in the eighties.

As I walked out of the Arcand Hotel onto the busy street, I could hardly believe I was finally in Lourdes. It had been nearly a year since my first meeting with Samarah, when she channeled Mary's message to me. Now, here I was in this beautiful historical place wondering what would unfold for me during my week stay. The words of the Blessed Mother were ringing in my ears when she said, "The memories will come. You know, in some ways it's like wanting an experience so much you're concentrating and it's like any magical rainbow. If you're watching on a rainy day saying, 'I want a rainbow, I want a rainbow, I want a rainbow,' it's not the same as if you say, 'Oh look, a rainbow!'" I couldn't go around looking for my rainbow because I might miss it altogether. I just had to go about the business at hand, focus on my duties as an Auxiliary and see what happened. Easier said than done.

We ate lunch at the Hotel D'Espagne at noon followed by some free time and rest. I must say I don't think too many of us rested. There was too much to do. We had to get our schedules, change into our work uniforms and try and find the malade we were assigned to. Since it was my first time, it was more than a little confusing for me.

At 3:45 we assembled in front of the hotels and processed to the Domaine for Mass at the Rosary Basilica. Still not at all sure of what I was supposed to be doing, I just followed. The streets were filled with Knights, Dames, Auxiliaries and caregivers tending to the malades seated in their voitures, or small hand-pulled carts. Usually a Knight would pull the voiture and two Auxiliaries would push. At this point I still hadn't found my malade, so I just helped out where I could.

Mass at the Basilica was beautiful. The Order of Malta had a choir that sang like angels throughout the service. Not having my bearings yet, I didn't realize that this was the Church that was built right on top of the Grotto, the place where my heart ached to be.

Once Mass was over, not wanting to get lost, I followed everyone back to the hotels. On the way back a Dame asked me if I had found my malade. I told her I hadn't, and she said she would help me. She looked at her schedule, which I eventually received, and told me that my malade was unable to come due to a passport problem.

Because there were so many of us on the trip, over four hundred, we were broken up into color-coded groups. I was beginning to realize how well organized this trip was and how much time, effort and love it took to put it all together. I was advised to check with one of my group leaders to see what I should do.

Dinner that night was at seven. I was running a little late, which is very unlike me, so when I arrived at the dining room there weren't very many empty seats. I really didn't know anyone anyway, so I just sat down at the first seat I could find. As I sat down at the table, I introduced myself to a very distinguished looking Knight, a beautiful silver haired woman and another lovely woman who seemed to be in her early thirties. After all of the introductions were over and we exchanged some small talk, I explained my dilemma to the Knight regarding my malade because I noticed that he was wearing a purple ribbon on his sleeve. We were in the same group.

As I was explaining my problem, everyone at the table started smiling. I was starting to wonder what was going on. I guess I shouldn't have been too surprised when he said to me, "Welcome, we have been looking for you. Let me re-introduce you to your malade." I looked over to the beautiful woman who was there with her daughter. As our eyes met again I felt that this was meant to be. Before I started putting pen to paper to write this book, I decided that I was not going to reveal anyone's name or their circumstances. Going on this Pilgrimage is a very personal and individual decision and I intend to protect everyone's privacy. As we all continued to enjoy our delicious meal, I silently thanked Mother Mary for seating me at the right table.

After dinner, because we had all been awake for over thirty-six hours by now, we called it a night. Breakfast was at 7:30 AM and we all needed our rest.

Friday, April 29, 2005

I found out at breakfast that my "new" malade had been on a waiting list. She was able to come at the last minute because of the confusion with the other malade's passport. Although I am not going to mention her name or her medical condition, I will say that if nothing else happened to me on this trip, it would have been complete for me just to have met her. She was the epitome of love and grace and I felt honored to be of service to her. You also couldn't help but to see the love and devotion her daughter felt for her. It was true for all family members or loved ones who came here as caregivers. To come so far, and for some with so much difficulty, to bring their loved one to this sacred place, to come before Our Lady with such faith and hope, praying in their own way for a cure in whatever form that took, I felt blessed to be a part of it all.

The Basilica of the Rosary

"The Esplanade" the statue of Our Lady Crowned

"The Grotto" where the Blessed Mother appeared to Bernadette

After breakfast we had some free time before the next organized event. This was my chance to go to the Grotto. As I headed towards the Domaine, my heart was pounding. With the Blessed Mother's words still fresh in my head, my mind still wouldn't stop spinning. "What is going to happen when I arrive? Will the skies open up and angels start to sing? Will the people there know who I am? Will I remember? Or will nothing happen?"

The area around the Grotto is roped off with signs requesting silence. As I approached, my eyes fell upon the small niche where the apparitions took place. It seemed so small, nestled in the gray rocks under the huge Church. I gazed at the beautiful statue of Our Lady. The Grotto was filled with hundreds of people, malades in their voitures, groups of pilgrims praying the Rosary, people of all nationalities kneeling on the ground in silent prayer. I stood there transfixed. With all of the hundreds of people there in the Grotto, I felt like I was the only one. Alone with the Divine Mother. I have never felt such love and peace. I fell to my knees and began to weep.

I don't know how long I had been on my knees before I looked up and saw a line forming, waiting to walk through the Grotto. I got up and joined them. As I walked through the Grotto, running my hands over the smooth wet rock, I suddenly noticed the spring that Bernadette had uncovered. I could feel my breathing begin to deepen. I wanted so desperately to remember my life as Bernadette. As a hynotherapist, I realized that you can't force past life memories. I would just have to wait and see what did or did not happen. As I walked through and then under the statue of Our Lady, a great sense of calm and serenity overtook me. I felt deeply connected to this place. I was brought here for a reason.

After lunch we were scheduled to go to the baths. There are fourteen stone baths where the sick and well alike are immersed in the Lourdes water. The baths are situated about two hundred yards past the Grotto. Half are reserved for men and the other half for women. Outside the baths is usually someone reciting the Rosary. Each bathing room has its own dressing room with curtains. The rooms have two benches and hooks on each sidewall. Three or four volunteer assistants help the bather to undress while covered with a large cotton robe. The attendants are very respectful and helpful. At no time is the bather exposed. While waiting, the bather sits wrapped in their robe on the bench and prays until it is their turn. The bather then goes through a curtain to the bath. The bath is a long, narrow stone tub with three steps down to it. Three attendants assist you, two on either side holding the bather's arms, while the third prays with you. While still covered, the bather is wrapped in a huge linen cloth, which is very cold and then walks down the steps to the stone bath. They can then sit or lie in the water or simply walk to the other end. There is a statue of the Blessed Mother at the end of the bath. You are asked if you would like to say a prayer. When the bather is finished they are again wrapped in a large covering and are brought back to the dressing room where they are helped to get dressed. The volunteers who work in the baths are experienced and very skillful at working with bathers in wheelchairs and stretchers. The whole process is very modest and prayerful.

On the way to the baths everyone was commenting on the weather. It was another warm, sunny and beautiful day. As we approached the baths, there seemed to be some confusion. We were scheduled for this time but it appeared that they wouldn't be able to accommodate all of us. After some discussion, most of us decided to return on another day. I was thrilled because my malade and her daughter were able to go in. When they emerged from the bath, the look on their faces said it all. Although physical healing is rare, people's spirits are usually blessed.

When we returned from the baths there was a little downtime before dinner. It was suggested that at meals we all try to sit at different tables so we could have the chance to meet as many people as possible. Being a shy person, I thought that this would be very difficult for me, but I found the opposite to be true. No matter where I sat, I felt welcomed. Although most people at the table knew each other, they all included me as if we were all old friends. I never once felt uncomfortable. After dinner I made it another early night.

Saturday, April 30, 2005

Breakfast at seven. After breakfast we assembled outside to process to the Domaine for 8:30 Mass at the Grotto. We would meet in front of the hotels, where our Knight would be ready with the voiture for our malade. We would all form in our color-coded groups and process through the busy streets filled with tourists, buses, people on their way to work and, of course, the many gift shops dotted along the route to the Domaine.

Once again it was another beautiful day. Mass was celebrated outdoors right in the Grotto. By this time, I was pretty familiar with the area. There have been several basilicas, churches and chapels built within the Domaine. When the construction of a church was first discussed, it was decided to build a crypt into the center of the Massabielle Rock and a church whose choir would be directly above the site of the apparitions. The work started in October of 1862. Four years later the Crypt was completed. On May 21, 1866 it was inaugurated, in the presence of Bernadette. Inside the Crypt are four chapels, dedicated to the Sacred Heart, Saint Peter, Saint Joseph and Saint John the Evangelist. Above the altar is a statue of the Madonna and Child.

The Upper Basilica was built directly above the Crypt. It was opened to the public in 1871 and in 1874 Pope Pius IX raised it to the rank of minor basilica. Inside there are ten chapels dedicated to saints who had a particular devotion to Our Lady. The Chapel of Saint Germain contains three large marble slabs on which the dates of the eighteen apparitions and the words of the Blessed Mother have been engraved. There are also a series of stained glass windows telling the story of Our Lady's apparitions to Bernadette and of the pilgrimage to Lourdes. Inside also stands a statue of the Crowned Virgin that was placed in the basilica during the ceremony of the coronation of Our Lady of Lourdes.

In 1875 it was decided to build a new church dedicated to the Rosary. It took six years to complete. During the construction it was necessary to dig into the rock and concrete foundations that were sunk below the level of the Gave River. The church was inaugurated in

1889, consecrated in 1901 and raised to the rank of basilica in 1926 by Pope Pius XI. The dome of the church bears a crown and a cross commemorating the coronation of Our Lady of Lourdes. The tympanum above the portal depicts Our Lady and the Infant Jesus giving the Rosary to Saint Dominic. To the left is a medallion of Pope Leo XIII and to the right a medallion of Pope Pius XII. When you enter the basilica, the vaulted ceiling of the choir has a beautiful painting of Our Lady of Lourdes. There are fifteen side chapels, each of which have a mosaic depicting one of the Mysteries of the Rosary.

During Mass, the choir once again sounded like angels from Heaven. It was a very moving service. Although I was trying to fight the temptation, I was still looking for signs from Mother Mary, something to confirm Samarah's channeling and my growing feeling that there was something very special waiting to reveal itself to me. I was looking for my rainbow.

After Mass my malade wanted to go to the Poor Clare Convent that was near our hotel for the Adoration of the Blessed Sacrament. I can't express how much I admired her. She never complained and was always concerned that we were working too hard. I would have done anything for her.

After we left the Convent, she was feeling a little tired so we brought her back to the hotel. Our malades are always our first priority but if they wanted some down time it gave us a little free time. I took that opportunity to go back to the Grotto. I couldn't stay away, it seemed as though an unseen force kept drawing me back. I stayed so long that I was able to recite the Hail Mary in French just by listening to it being repeated by the priest. I was in Heaven.

Later that day I found out that the first-time Knights, Dames and Candidates went on a walk called "The Footsteps of Bernadette," where they were taken to Bernadette's home, where her father had his mill, to the one room home where they all lived during the apparitions, and all around the important sites of her young life. I was so excited because that was exactly what I wanted to experience. Sadly, I learned that because of the extreme heat wave we were having, this journey would probably not be repeated. I was heartbroken, but I realized that everything happens for a reason.

I also used some of my free time to buy bottles to fill up with the Lourdes water. Everyone who knew I was going to Lourdes had asked me to bring them home some water. To the left of the Grotto are spigots where you can go and either fill up bottles with water or just cup your hands and drink. Many people were just pouring it over themselves. All the water is from the spring. There is no end to it; it just continues to flow.

That night we all went to the candlelight procession on the Esplanade in the Domaine. In the center of the Esplanade is a beautiful statue of Our Lady Crowned. At dusk, the pilgrims congregate for the Rosary procession. Each of us was given a small white candle. Slowly we processed around the Esplanade as the Rosary was recited by an announcer in French, English, Spanish, Italian, Polish and German. After each decade, everyone sang the "Lourdes Hymn." Thousands of pilgrims lifted their candles in unison as we sang "Ave Maria." Flames burning from our candles and in our hearts, all for the love of Our Lady. What a beautiful sight.

Sunday, May 1, 2005

May, Mary's month, what a perfect time to be in Lourdes. After last nights candlelight ceremony I decided to stop looking for signs. I was having an experience of a lifetime. Imagine me, in France, coming to this extraordinary place. The beauty and peacefulness of Lourdes was beyond words. I knew that this was going to be the first of many pilgrimages for me.

After breakfast we assembled outside with our groups to process to the Pius X Basilica for 9:30 Mass. In 1956, as the number of pilgrims grew, it was decided that a new basilica was needed. Due to the lack of room within the Domaine, it was decided to build an underground basilica, which was consecrated in March 1958, marking the centenary of the apparitions. It seats 25,000 people but can hold 30,000. The structure is oval shaped and made of concrete and supported by 58 triangular posts that form 29 porticoes. Lining the walls are huge portraits of saints at least ten feet high and hanging high above the floor are huge screens that show the words of the hymns being sung in French, English, Italian, Spanish and German.

As our angelic choir sang, I was caught up by the majesty of it all. Thousands of people gathered in this one place to worship God and sing hymns to Our Lady. Looking around at all the portraits of the saints, I realized that I was seated directly across from the portrait of Saint Bernadette. At that moment I stopped singing. Something in my reality was starting to shift. Suddenly I was losing the awareness of the people and the singing and everything going on around me. What was happening? Everything seemed to be going in slow motion until time just seemed to stand still. Then I noticed the presence of another spirit within me. It wasn't overtaking me but rather it seemed to be merging deep within my soul. It was a beautiful feeling, so I wasn't frightened. I then heard these words resound throughout every cell in my body. "Awaken, we have come to continue the work of Our Lady." I felt my heart stop, but at the same time I had never felt more alive. "Oh my God!" Tears started streaming down my face. "Oh, my God! I know you. I know who you are." My heart was racing now; my mind was spinning. "All this time I was waiting for a sign from the Blessed Mother, but it's you. You have been with me all along. You brought me to this beautiful place to reawaken my soul. It's you, Bernadette! Oh, my God." I could hardly sit still; her words were still pulsating in my heart. I looked around to see if anyone had noticed what had just happened to me. Everyone was still singing, Mass was proceeding as usual. How could they not know what had just taken place? Didn't they realize what just happened? Couldn't they feel this energy coming from me? Nothing had changed for them, but I knew that my life would never be the same again.

It was at that moment I realized that I didn't need any memories from a past life. I didn't need to remember my life as Bernadette. Her spirit has just been reawakened in me. She has told me that together we must finish what she started. Our Lady has much more for us to do. It's time. Everything inside of me was crying out, "Yes!" When I stopped looking for my rainbow, it found me.

When the service ended, I was still in a daze. I looked around and realized that everyone was touched by their own personal emotions. Ever since my channelings almost a year ago I knew that my life was going to change. Now, it is real to me. What I've been waiting for has finally happened and it is like Mother Mary said, "Once you know the truth, no one can take it away from you. The truth shall set you free." I spent a lot of time at the Grotto that day, praying and thanking Bernadette and Our Lady.

This is what I wrote in my journal that night.

I was blessed with a beautiful gift today. During Mass at the Pius X Basilica, I saw the rainbow! As the Mass was going on, Bernadette came and spoke these words to me. "Awaken, we have come to continue the work of Our Lady." Imagine how I felt. Tears filled my eyes. I felt Bernadette deep within my soul. She is with me. We are one. Two separate lives but one soul. I was waiting to hear your voice, Mother but it came from Bernadette. How perfect! I now know and feel the truth. My mind, body and spirit are now joined in the truth. I have longed for this for so many years. It's all real! My heart is so full of love. Thank you, Mother. Thank you, Bernadette. I will help to continue the work of Our Lady. I'm so glad I said, "Yes."

Monday, May 2, 2005

Too excited to sleep, I laid awake most of the night. Breakfast was at 7:30 AM so I decided to get up around 5:00 AM and take a quick shower. Our rooms were very small so I tried to be very quiet so I wouldn't wake my roommate, a really nice woman from New Jersey.

Today we were attending Mass at the Sacré Coeur Parish in Lourdes. The church where Bernadette was christened was destroyed by fire in 1905 and in its place a public garden was made with a war memorial dedicated to the soldiers of the First and Second World

Wars. A newer and larger parish church was built nearby. Bernadette's baptismal font was placed in the new church.

During Mass I received a message from the Blessed Mother and Bernadette thanking me for taking this leap of faith and for traveling such a distance. I then asked Mary, "What now? What's next?" and Our Lady replied, "What do you think I was preparing you for? I have taught you well. You are ready. I am with you always. Do not fear. All is as it should be. Just follow. I love you." My heart pounded with love.

After Mass there was a picnic scheduled at Grottes de Betharram, a short bus ride from the church, but my malade was too tired to attend. As Mother Mary had said, things would happen with serendipity and as it would happen, one of our team leaders offered to take our little group on a walking tour of the footsteps of Bernadette. This was the very same tour that I missed and had so wanted to experience. We had a wheelchair for our malade, so everyone agreed to go. What a blessing. We saw Bernadette's first home and her father's mill. There was a little museum of sorts with her christening gown on display and a small replica she had made of the Grotto. There were family portraits hanging on the walls and we were able to go upstairs to her bedroom. Because of her asthma, Bernadette had the bed closest to the window. We also went to the cachot where the Soubirous family lived at the time of the apparitions. All the while I was thankful that I wasn't pressuring myself to remember aspects of that life. It wasn't necessary anymore.

As I mentioned, the weather was unusually hot for that time of year and the extreme heat really bothered my malade. After we arrived back at the hotel after our wonderful tour, my malade wanted to go to her room to rest. This meant that once more I had some free time. I decided I would return to the Grotto and try to get into the baths.

I had mixed feeling about going into the baths. I knew in my mind that it was rare that people received physical healings but under the circumstances I thought maybe I might be an exception.

I was born with congenital cataracts and at age twenty-one, I began surgery. Because I was so young to have cataract surgery, they had to operate on each eye two separate times. Twelve years later, I suffered from a detached retina in my left eye. After three unsuccessful surgeries, I had to confront the fact that I would only have sight in my right eye. The problem was that my right eye already had three holes in the retina that were treated at the time of my first retinal surgery. A few years went by and the retina detached in my right eye as well. Because I knew what signs to look for, I took immediate action and had a successful surgery performed at Massachusetts Eye and Ear Infirmary.

What would happen when I went into the baths? Would I miraculously regain the sight in my left eye? After all, look who I was supposed to be. If a miracle didn't happen to me then to whom? But the words of Mother Mary were still ringing in my ears, "The water at Lourdes continues to have the purity and the grace of unconditional love, and so it continues to flow in order to offer that to everyone." She went on to explain that people still have their contracts to fulfill, things to learn and work out. No matter who I had been in a past life, I knew that my present life was filled with different challenges and lessons. Although I would love to receive a physical healing, I knew deep in my heart that no matter who I had been in a past life, in this life I would get no special treatment, no free ride. That is Universal Law. After all, I had received my miracle yesterday from Bernadette herself.

I was in luck. The line waiting to go into the baths wasn't very long. As I sat on the benches, weaving my way up the line, praying to Our Lady, I couldn't help but think of the past year and all the circumstances that brought me to this beautiful place. Meeting Samarah, the channelings, being able to come with the Knights of Malta, everything just seemed so right, like it was all pre-ordained.

It was now my turn to go into the small curtained area to prepare for the baths. The women volunteering couldn't have been nicer or more respectful. They kept me completely covered while I disrobed. There were six of us waiting in this small area, each of us with our own special intentions. I was so moved by it all I started to cry softly, my love for Our Lady was so great. As I looked into the eyes of the other women, I could tell they felt the same. We were all sharing a silent bond.

As the curtain opened three women appeared to assist me. My white cotton robe was replaced with a very cold linen cloth. As I walked down the three stairs, being held on either side, a feeling of complete and total surrender came over me. I walked over and kissed the statue of the Blessed Mother and was then guided by the two women to sit. The third woman was in constant prayer. As I sat in the Lourdes water, all I could feel was total peace. I knew that no matter what happened to me in these brief moments, everything was going to be fine. Whether or not I regained the eyesight in my eye no longer mattered to me anymore. I was completely overcome by the love of Our Lady. With tears streaming down my face, I was lifted up and preceded to kiss Mary's statue one more time before leaving the bath. Climbing back up the stairs, I was again put into my robe and escorted through the curtain. Another volunteer was waiting to help me dress. I couldn't believe it when I heard this beautiful French woman speak to me. Her voice sounded exactly like Samarah's when she is channeling Mother Mary. I was so moved that I gave her a huge hug. She then gave me a kiss on each cheek. Smiling, she looked deeply into my eyes. I realized that she knew exactly what was in my heart. I felt the presence of Our Lady. It is an experience I will never forget. It's really remarkable, for as wet as you are when you get out of the baths, while dressing and subsequently leaving, by the time you are outside you are almost completely dry! I remained at the Grotto for a while before returning to the hotel. I don't even remember my walk back. I didn't have a care in the world. I was in heaven.

Tuesday, May 3, 2005

I knew that this would be my last full day in Lourdes. In one way I didn't want to leave, but I knew Mother Mary had plans for me that my soul had agreed to even before my birth. The joy in my heart was full to overflowing, realizing that such an important gift was given to me. I was to continue the work I had started when I lived as Bernadette. I knew that with Our Lady's guidance it would be accomplished.

After breakfast we all assembled for closing Mass in the Upper Basilica. Each service held in the Domaine was made more beautiful by the glorious sounds of the choir. When Mass ended, my malade wanted to say the Stations of the Cross. The Way of the Cross entails a walk of about one mile. There are one hundred and fifteen figures in bronzed cast iron somewhat larger than life size making up the fourteen stations. In some areas it is very steep and could prove a little difficult even for an able bodied person.

There is another Way of the Cross in an area that is shaded by trees and is on level ground. We decided this one would be more appropriate. The Stations are engraved in lava and set into the wall that runs alongside the River Gave. What a beautiful setting. As the priest was leading us through the Stations, he was accompanied by the melodious songs of the birds that are always flying around the Grotto. It was like they were there with only one intention, to sing honor and praise to Mary. The love in their song was very evident.

Built nearby this beautiful spot is St. Bernadette's Chapel. This Chapel marks the exact spot from which Bernadette saw the Apparition for the last time. The church was built in 1986 and dedicated on March 25, 1988. It can hold up to 5,000 people. It is basically an amphitheatre in design, with mobile partitions that can be used to separate the church by approximately two thirds to one third. The whole area is called the Meadow or Prairie. It was very emotional for me when I looked over at the Grotto from that spot because I knew that this could be the last time I saw the place where the Blessed Mother appeared to Bernadette all those years ago. Tears of both sadness and joy filled my eyes.

At lunch I was graced with the companionship of a very lovely woman who happened to be the very first chairperson of the Order of Malta Pilgrimages twenty years ago. When lunch was over, we happened to be the last two people at the table. She mentioned that she would like to go to another hotel where they formerly stayed in order to leave a note for an old friend. She was concerned though, because the walk was long and uphill and she was feeling a little unsteady. As you know by now, nothing happens by accident. My malade was tired and wanted to return to her room to rest, so my afternoon was free. I gladly volunteered my services and off we went. What a treat for me. As we walked, we talked a little about our lives, some of the other Pilgrimages, and life in general. When our time together was over, I thanked her for my special afternoon and I thanked Our Lady for arranging it all.

Dinner that night was bittersweet. No one wanted to leave, but we all knew it was time to venture back out into the real world. What a week it had been. The weather was unseasonably warm and sunny, the food at every meal was delicious and the gift I received from meeting all the malades and their caregivers was priceless. Such love and faith they expressed, and each went home with a healing, if not physical, surely spiritual.

After dinner we were treated to some great entertainment. Some of the younger Auxiliary put on a musical skit. It was a good-natured roasting of the Knights and Dames. There was singing, dancing and joke telling and no one enjoyed it more than the Knights and Dames themselves. When it ended, a lot of us said our goodbyes because we knew tomorrow would be quite hectic. As I looked over at my malade and her daughter, I thanked Our Lady for putting them in my life. They will remain in my heart forever.

Wednesday, May 4, 2005

Breakfast at 7:30 AM then boarding the buses to depart for the airport around 8:30 AM. A few more last minute hugs and goodbyes. On the bus ride to the airport, as we rode through the beautiful countryside, I could feel that both Our Lady and Bernadette were telling me that whatever lay ahead it was still my choice. No matter what our sacred contract is, we always have the choice to say no, not this time, but I knew what my answer was with no hesitation. It was a resounding yes!

I was going home to chronicle everything that had happened. The Blessed Mother didn't want me to share this until I had confidence in what I was writing. Well, I certainly do now. I will tell my story because Our Lady said that by telling mine it will help others to find theirs.

As we boarded the plane for the long flight home, I said my goodbyes to France and to Our Lady of Lourdes, knowing deep in my heart that they would both be with me forever.

Chapter VII

Before I left for Lourdes, I learned that Samarah would be making another visit to New England, so I made an appointment to see her on May 25, 2005. There was a bond growing between us that was lovely. Introduced by Mother Mary, we were becoming good friends.

As we greeted each other, it was hard to believe that so much time had passed since our last encounter. It was wonderful to see her. Before we started the session, I told her the experience of my awakening by Bernadette. She was very happy for me. I knew that Samarah and I were brought together for a purpose. We had both said yes to Mother Mary.

After Samarah's usual prayers of preparation, this was the channeling that followed. Mother Mary speaks first:

"It's so lovely to see you again, and so lovely to feel your clarity, your knowing and your faith. I want to say, 'solid as a rock,' but that sounds like a commercial (laughter). It's so beautiful. You seem so peaceful and excited simultaneously."

"Yes, exactly."

"And everything now just falls into place. People will say, 'Does that mean you'll know where you'll be two weeks from now?' No, it means that each day you know that you are right where you are supposed to be. When it was taught that you were given daily bread it wasn't taught that you were given monthly or yearly bread. It was said daily bread. That's to help you to stay in the present. Right here, right now, absolutely sure that you are exactly where you need to be. And if that changes and a bell rings, you'll go to something else. So no matter what we say today, it's just about being with you and saying thank you."

"You're thanking me?"

"Yes. You see, without your permission and your willingness you and I wouldn't be sitting here. I think as the next part of your life starts to unfold and the book starts to come together even more clearly, there is permission and there is willingness. And what is the story of Bernadette? It's the willingness and also that she did not listen to the priest for permission. She listened to what we will call a higher authority. And so the lesson of that is also part of the story. Permission comes from within. You gave yourself permission to hear the truth of your life, to feel the story of your life unfolding, to follow you heart. The reason that that is so important is because all over our universe right now we still have those who are waiting for someone else to give them permission. That keeps them childlike in a way. And it's all right if you are a child. Yet if you are growing into your beingness it's time to say, 'You mean I had permission all along?' and then to breath in the scary part, like that moment I said to you it might be nice for you to go to Lourdes. And you said to yourself, 'What me, how? How could I possibly go to Lourdes? Do you know how much that costs?' (Laughter) And yet you gave yourself permission and you offered your willingness and now look what has occurred. I know you know all this but I put it on the tape because as you are writing, this too will be woven into the story, your willingness and your permission, Samarah's willingness and permission, and of course Bernadette's willingness and permission. Part of the reason for that is that people still think that something like that can never happen to them, that they're just an ordinary Joe. To bring through the story that Bernadette was just an ordinary girl, not a renowned scholar, in fact she couldn't even read, really brings home that everyone is both ordinary and extraordinary. This journey is about recognizing that and realizing that if you are willing and give yourself permission to take in this thought that you too are here for a reason beyond your job and beyond this and beyond that.

"Within you lies this beautiful unfolding map and sometimes you have to take a step into the unknown because the map doesn't show you everything. It just says to do the next thing. When you went to Lourdes you didn't know what would happen. And you didn't know for sure and absolute that something would happen. Yet you were willing to go. You gave yourself permission to go. The miracle and the mystery that you are so woven with right now happened not because you were trying so hard, not because you were concentrating with all your being, but because you opened yourself to being present and trusting that the next part of the map would show up when it was supposed to."

"And it did."

"Tell me a little more."

"The faith of the people there was so profound. And the love of the caregivers is also very profound."

"Yes, you really get to feel love there, don't you, and faith. These too are part of the story. When you say the word faith, people have a variety of responses to that, but when you feel your own faith it's almost like there is a special tune that allows you to then feel the faith of others. You can say, I know your faith because I have found mine. It might look a little different here or there but I know this energy of faith. There at Lourdes if you think of the millions of people who have gone there over the years it's like a river of faith that runs through Lourdes. Anyone who goes, I believe their faith is increased and renewed even if they don't get exactly what they were looking for. They feel all of those hearts yearning to be in the presence of the Divine."

"That was very evident. As people walked through the Grotto, they touched the rocks to feel the energy."

"Yes, to feel closer, to realize that this life has both the ordinary and the extraordinary simultaneously available to your willingness and permission and faith."

"You are still appearing to the visionaries in Medjugorje?"

"Yes, I'm still quite busy, yes." (Laughter)

"Have you been to other places?"

"Well, you know I show up in a lot of different ways and some of them are more visible or obvious and some, shall we say, get more press. The truth is Mary I will be here for as long as I am needed. I will show up any way I know how to, including right now in Circles of

Wisdom (the place where channeling is taking place). The idea of having these apparitions again and again in office buildings or wherever is to remind people that the extraordinary is here. The Divine is here. You don't just sit in your cubicle at work and that's it. There is more. So, myself and many others come as reminders that there is more for those who have eyes to see and ears to hear."

"Will that be happening more and more? Will Ascended Masters be coming down more than they usually have?"

"Well, I'll tell you what's happening. Ascended Masters like Bernadette are coming to call on the ordinary every day and also on the extraordinary individuals around the world to bring them together in books, films, and music and in many other ways. So, it's not like you have to travel to Lourdes or Medjugorje to have these experiences. Your book will reach many, many people and how lovely is that? And yes, more and more of the Masters are coming but they come to tap on your shoulder and that one's shoulder and this one's shoulder. If those others give permission and are willing, they work together to create all sorts of other ways to let people know what is possible."

"So, they're working through us."

"Yes, they're working with people and through people in a sort of Divine partnership."

"How did I reincarnate from France to New England?"

"First of all, you decided that America would be much more open to these next things you wanted to do. So you decided to come to America where there is much more freedom of all sorts of expressions."

"And I picked my parents and my surroundings?"

"Yes."

"Did my spirit guides help me?"

"Do not forget that when you leave the human realm, before you come back, you know everything I know. To say that we help you isn't quite right. We are with you and say, 'All right, I know what I will do. I will go back to America this time.' (Laughter) You know that I'm making light of it, but it's really more like you say, 'All right, I will go back to America but I do think that being a woman would be a good idea rather than a man because of the energy and let me see what else.' And so you do that, you create the environment that will lead you to be where you are right now. It's sort of like you leave off and you come back and you say, 'Oh, what I would like to see now is how I could....' and you move on from there. It's a little more expansive than the idea of the karmic wheel, that you were bad here so now you'll be good there. It's more creative and lovely than that. You think that if you came back as a woman who could not read or write, it would be difficult to write a book so you won't do it that way. (Laughter) Then you create from that perspective."

"The feeling that I'm getting from Bernadette is that she was very sad that a lot of people didn't believe her."

"Well, yes. Let us put you in her shoes for a moment. I will tell you some things but as you are writing she will tell you some things too. I love the purity of that and the confidence you will have in that. Imagine if you came back from your experience at Lourdes, and I know you have not told many people, but image that everyone that you told looked at you and said you were out of your mind, ridiculed you and basically treated you as a lunatic. What would you do then, if you were Bernadette? You would shut yourself away, retreat inside yourself and say, 'Well, I do know the truth. I will be with Our Lady. I will be in this truth. I will just live my life without saying much of anything because no one believes me at this time.' The nice thing about this life, Mary, is that even though you only told a few people, they were happy and excited for you and very encouraging. Now you are opening to more experiences like writing this book and to being the voice that you could not be then."

"I got that feeling when I was there. It was like Bernadette was saying to me, 'Now it's your turn to continue the message as it was meant to be told.'"

"Yes, that is exactly right and you will hear her even more now. From time to time, just as you are asking me, ask her and listen for the answer and you will hear her. But realize that from time to time there will be those out there who will tell you that you are a lunatic."

"Oh, I'm sure that's going to happen."

"But I will tell you that Samarah and I sat down with each other in the beginning and she said that to me and I told her, 'You know what dear, just decide that it does not matter and know that you are surrounded by people who love you and appreciate you and respect you.' It has been so and Samarah has traveled to many places and I do believe it will be so for you as well, because the other thing that you chose was to come now, here, in this world where on TV now you can watch "Medium." (Laughter) Right? And people are much more accepting of these phenomenon and that is because they are so hungry and curious while still not quite at the willingness and permission stage. But they are curious and fascinated, and so you have chosen a time for this book to come out when there will be a great interest. This is partly because you are writing it from your heart and not beating anyone in the head with it. You really aren't. You are simply saying, this is the story that I know and that I have lived, and it will be so pure and clear and filled with love that many people will just eat it up."

"The message that we want to give is for people to take back their Divine Power."

"Exactly, exactly."

"I've read that when you came to Bernadette you asked her to tell the priests that you wanted people to process and to have churches built at Lourdes. Is that correct? Could you clarify that?"

"I would be glad to. When I came to Bernadette, I told her that she was a child of God and that in her hands was the power of God as it was in the hands of all and that she needed no one to connect her to God. No priest, no church, nothing. By following her hearing and knowing the voice of truth that she would be led to a spring that no one would know about nor had found. When she found it, she would know that the spring of water, the water of light, the water of spirit, was absolutely true and real for her and for everyone. That is what I told her. Now, when she went to the priests and said all of that, they added a few things. Because let's face it, he didn't want to abdicate that responsibility and power that he felt. And also, in all fairness, he thought that people would begin to run around misunderstanding what had been said, taking it to mean they could do anything they liked because they were God. That might have happened in some cases because you were still working with a lot of immature souls at that time. And so he added a few extra lines to say let us have lots of churches and we will still have priests to help you through all of this. He also left out a few of the other parts. So no, I never asked to have churches built."

"This is going to surprise a lot of people but it needs to be told. That's why we're doing this."

"Exactly."

"Did you ask people to come in procession?"

"What I said at that time was to come and witness. Come and witness the spring of life that is here for all of you. Now, to make a procession, that was part of their way of celebrating and acknowledging what had happened and that was fine. You know that whether there is one person or a thousand in a line, the important thing is that if you are one of those, you are feeling your connection with God. If being in a procession helps you because you feel the power and the strength of so many in faith, that's fine. It is not a requirement. It's like the difference between saying "Hail Mary" because you are filled with love and saying "Hail Mary" because you are worried about the sin you have just committed. Do you see the difference? What I say is, say a "Hail Mary" because you are loving yourself and perhaps me and all of God, not because you are worried that you will be punished and put in a black fiery place or something."

"It's not exactly the words that are being said but the feeling that goes with it."

"It is the feeling and the realizing that you are no longer being punished. Actually, you were never being punished by some fearsome God who wanted you to do this but not this, that but not that. It was to realize that you are perfect and that your perfection is this connection with God that you can feel and follow. That is why in some ways it is wonderful that we have Buddhists and Christians and Sufis. They have all found many ways to express this connection to the Divine. Live the truth of that because all of those teachings have at their root the belief that we are all one. People forgot that part and say, 'you know, if you're not this, then...' and all that stuff. The lesson about Bernadette is really all about the purity of being one with the Divine."

"The Catholic Church is going to be a little upset when this comes out."

"Well, I would suggest you look at it this way, Mary. The church does not read the book, people do. Rather than worrying about some group called the church as you create your book, just know and dwell in this energy of love that you are and say, 'I offer this with my love.' Whatever happens will happen. There are many very beautiful Catholic priests and nuns who really know everything we are speaking of right now. And yet their willingness so far to go a little farther has not yet occurred. You know the old saying, 'Know ye the truth and the truth shall set you free.' Not everyone wants freedom because with that comes responsibility. To hear your own voice and not someone else saying, 'All right Mary, let's see what you have done.' All right, that will be four Our Fathers and three Hail Mary's. (Laughter) You know? Some people still like to be treated like children. I've said my four Our Fathers and three Hail Mary's and on I go. It is much more beautiful but also more complex than that."

"I always thought that it was funny that you asked Bernadette to build churches."

"Yes, it always felt wrong to you. I am glad that you brought it up because while you are writing you might read something else, but always check with Bernadette. She will set you straight."

"A lot of people are going to say that Bernadette was a saint. Why would she come back?"

"What do they think a saint does, just go up there and play a harp for the rest of eternity? How boring would that be?" (Laughter)

"People don't realize that even Jesus reincarnated."

"Absolutely."

"And you, too."

"And me too, sure. If you live in this limited box then you must have limiting thoughts to go in your limited box, and that's okay but part of what all these beautiful books, music and movies are doing is to show people that there is more out there and that there are many, many different creators right now like yourself that are aligning their energies with the energies of beings who want this next part to continue. Oh right, you think, well Bernadette was a saint and she did what she did, but if her mission was not complete in the sense of really letting people know their extra-divine nature then she would not be content up there playing her harp."

"So she decided to come back as me?"

"Yes. I want to tell you one other thing. When a soul goes home and then reincarnates, the soul itself in a way is larger than the human being. So right now you are not the only Bernadette. She has put some of her spirit right now around the world in various forms. You are one of the very few that was in agreement about writing this story starting with Lourdes and coming forward. So it is for you to do this writing. Okay?"

"Yes, I understand that such a great soul would come back into more than just one person."

"You are one of a few, yes."

"There is a big controversy about the fact that Jesus married Mary Magdelene. Is that true?"

(A big smile acknowledging agreement.)

"Did they just have one child, Sarah?"

(Again, another show of agreement.)

"And their bloodline continues?"

"Isn't that comforting?"

"Yes it is. It's hard for me to understand why people just can't get that."

"It's the box. You know the Catholic Church and many others have done a great sales job. And if you really want to stay in that box and just go through life just saying three Hail Mary's and four Our Fathers for every sin you commit, still going to Heaven, then you are willing to accept a few other things too. You see?"

"Besides Jesus, you had other children?"

"Yes. You see, isn't that lovely?"

"Yes it is. Is there anything else you would want me to say in the book?"

"Well right now I would really love for you to focus on your conversation with Bernadette in the book. Did you take many pictures while you were there?"

"Yes, a few."

"Take a look at putting together some pictures because some of what you are doing of course is telling the story but you are also helping to put people there so they get to feel the Grotto, to feel the energy of that place. Use pictures of the processions, whatever you feel drawn to. Meanwhile you are sort of putting those together. I also think you should begin to put together your chapters. Some of it, Mary, quite definitely needs to include your walk of faith."

"As a child to now?"

"Yes, yes so there will be the current trip to Lourdes, there is Bernadette's experience at Lourdes and there is Samarah's involvement. You see, you have many events to weave together."

"In the past I have done some automatic writing and I have contacted Saint Germain."

"Yes, Saint Germain is really all about transmutation. Part of what you are doing now is transmuting fear, and transmuting this box, for want of a better word. This prison that people have allowed themselves to be put into and that they have been kept in by not only the Catholic Church but by many other groups. You are transmuting so that the walls of that prison fall down. That leaves people looking around but not necessarily taking the next steps and so the book then gives them the opportunity to look at things differently. In that sense shall we say, you are using the violet flame in your life. That is why Saint Germain is so connected to you."

"Is there a better way to connect to Bernadette too? Should I try automatic writing or should I just be open?"

"Both, absolutely, just ask her the next time because it will be a while before I see you again. You can just make a list of questions for

Bernadette and, trust me, you will get all the answers directly from her spirit to yours to put in the book in the different chapters as it seems to be just right, absolutely."

"This is wonderful."

"Oh Mary, it is. It is so healing for you, for me, for everyone when you really live your faith and are not restrained or contained or bound by anyone. That is the liberation of Bernadette. That is really what you are doing. You are liberating the spirit of Bernadette from the box the Church wants to put her in and the life in which she was also restricted."

"That's what I felt. Like she would have liked to do something else with her life but the Church almost forced her into the convent."

"Of course, but remember what a young girl she was. What other choices did she have? To be illiterate, what could she do? And so this time…. All right Mary, (Laughter) you know you have no such restrictions as that and so it is the liberation of Bernadette and the liberation of that luminous experience. It does not belong to the Catholic Church. It does not belong to any church and in a funny way it does not even belong to Bernadette. When you have something like that liberation, it belongs to everyone."

"I just feel honored to be able to do this, that I said, 'Yes,' that I agreed."

"Yes, you agreed. You said, good job I'll take my mission. We will go down there this time but I do not want to be illiterate and I do not want to be in the convent and I do not want to live in France, but I will visit. I do not want to live there because I want to go to a country where women have for instance, more liberation and so, good job. I think the greatest sign of joy and knowingness is that gentle humility. Samarah does not want me to say this out loud, but she also feels the same thing, feels very humbled by how this happened, and that too tells you that this is not some ego trying to do anything. It is the liberation of light and the liberation of Spirit. And it is really your divine inheritance."

"Wow! That's all I can say."

"Yes Mary I am so excited for all that is unfolding for you."

"Thank you. I will continue to call on you and Bernadette."

"Yes, she is right here with you. It is very much like the way I came to Samarah. And that is it, the partnership is there. You allowed the door to be opened and so she will be with you the rest of your life. How lovely is that?"

"More than words, lovely. I surprised my whole family when I told them I was going to Lourdes. I was in that box, but I knew it was something I had to do."

"You see, going from the box to that openness, willingness and permission is absolutely an essential part of the story because when you are helping people come out of the box you needed to have been in it for a while also. They will see that in one day you said, 'Well, I'd like to go to Lourdes, I'm willing to go to Lourdes, I am going to Lourdes.' Just know that you are also creating with Saint Germain in the streams of light for your highest good."

"Thank you."

"May you just continue to have a beautiful, beautiful life where the faith that you are living is like the blossoms in spring. I see all flowers around you as the love that you are sharing and the faith that you are radiating and soon the book that will touch so many. So many, blessings my dear. Thank you so much."

"Namaste."

Chapter VIII

As Jimney Cricket so wonderfully put it, "A dream is a wish that your heart makes." We all have our own personal dreams. Maybe some of you think that it is too late for them to come true so you have stopped trying. Maybe you neatly packed them away long ago because life got in the way. What is your Sacred Contract? What is your passion? They are probably one and the same. Your Sacred Contract is a plan that you created for your life before you incarnated. With Divine guidance we each map out certain scenarios that will help our self and others in our spiritual growth. We choose our parents, siblings, children and close friends to have relationships with, all in an effort to fulfill our individual contracts. Each relationship we have has a purpose, from our most beloved friend to our worst enemy. We also incarnate with free will, the power of choice. Imagine you have the power to choose what your life will become. So why do so many of us give that power away? We give it away to our parents, friends, politicians, bosses, significant others and to our Churches.

Just for fun, try to suspend reality for a moment and recreate what might have been said and agreed upon during your meetings with your guides and teachers before you incarnated. What did you want to accomplish in this lifetime? What were your goals and dreams? What was the one thing you wanted most above all things to experience? Now, take a good long hard look at your life. Has it happened? Well, maybe now is the time to start taking steps to make it happen.

I think a lot of us are like Bernadette. She let people take away her power. She let them question and compromise her truth. And in the end, the Church changed the very truth she was here to tell us. Don't let anyone take away your power, your truth. Like you, I am still living an ordinary life. But we all have the opportunity to make our lives extraordinary. You and I are no different. There is no doubt that there is more to this life than what our five senses show us. Whether the sun is shinning or it is snowing doesn't change the nature of my knowing. It is like a steady heartbeat that is always with me and sees me through everything with beauty and love. We all have a journey to take. We all have a gift to give to the world and to ourselves. How will you make your life extraordinary?

I have been given a great gift. I have been given a second chance. I have been blessed with another opportunity to let the world know the true message given to Bernadette at Lourdes.

As I was writing this book, I realized how controversial it would be. I thought of the people who would be reading it and the effect it would have on them. I thought of the Catholic Church and how they would probably consider it blasphemous. I understood that there would be some who would think that I had lost my mind. None of that mattered. I knew what I had to do and nothing and no one would dissuade me. I was going to follow my heart.

This is why Our Lady came to Bernadette. She wanted the people to take back their Divine Power. She wanted to break the hold the priests held over them. She has come again with the same message. Mary wants you to remember who you are. You are a child of God. Believe in yourself. Live from your heart. It is time to stop blindly following what some institution programmed into you. If it doesn't feel right anymore, question it. You will always receive an answer. Start to look at things differently. Use what Mary calls your "soul sight." Guidance is always available, all you have to do is ask. Don't wait for someone else to give you permission.

Our Lady said that in many if not all of my lifetimes I have come to speak about freedom. Freedom is a choice. It is time to start taking responsibility for the direction your life is taking. Don't be afraid to stand up for what you believe in even though you may be challenged by those closest to you.

I believe that some of you who are reading these words are beginning your own revelation. It can be scary at first but trust what you are feeling. Be open. Listen to that small still voice inside of you. You don't have to travel to Lourdes or Medjugorje to have your own direct experience. All you need to do is be willing and give yourself permission to hear the truth of your life. As Mother Mary said, "Within you lies this beautiful unfolding map and sometimes you have to take a step into the unknown because the map doesn't show you everything." Take that leap of faith.

I am just the messenger. The message comes from Our Lady. Take back your Divine Power. It is yours but you have to claim it. Say "yes" to taking that first step outside the box and know that you will never walk alone.

Epilogue

"Welcome home."

"Thank You. It is nice to be back. Well, how did I do?"

"Nice try, you know the rules. You tell Us what you learned and then We throw in Our two cents."

"All right, just thought I would give it a shot. I always love going back down but I always forget how hard it can be. At first it is very difficult to adjust to being in such a small vessel but my connection to the Source was still so strong that it constantly sustained me.

"As I grew, I could still feel all the love and guidance surrounding me but as time went on, even though I had the love of my family and friends, I somehow felt that there was something missing. I started to lose my connection. I started to forget."

"You know that is the agreement you make before you start your new journey."

"I know but sometimes it gets so lonely."

"Those are the times you must listen for Us with all of your heart. You know We never leave you."

"But sometimes people can be so cruel and life can be so hard."

"Those are the times when you learn the most. What did you learn from those difficult times?"

"I learned to forgive."

"Go on."

"I realized that when people were being hurtful it really wasn't their fault. They were just afraid."

"Afraid of what?"

"Well, of just about everything! They were afraid of losing what they thought they could control like money, power, prestige and even love. They forgot that they didn't have to try to control anything. All they had to do was choose."

"Choose what?"

"To love."

"Is that what you learned?"

"Yes. I also learned that you don't have to try so hard. People take themselves so seriously. Life is to be enjoyed. When I realized that lesson, everything seemed to get easier and just sort of fell into place."

"What else?"

"I also began to start trusting myself more and to stop trying to please everyone else at my own expense. I started to do what I knew was right for me even though I knew that others might not agree with my decisions. When I started looking at myself differently I started seeing others with new insight. I realized that they had to do what was right for them too and if they did or said something that I didn't agree with, I should try to respect their point of view."

"Anything else?"

"I came to find out that we are all here for a reason. Everyone has their own itinerary. And no matter how big or small, no one's was more important than another's. Some people like to think that they were more important but in the long run we are all the same."

"Why do you think that people do not understand that?"

"I think it is because they have forgotten that they have the power to choose. They have forgotten that they have the power to take back the direction of their lives. That freedom is in their own hands. They have to start listening more to their hearts. Ultimately, they know what is right for them. They just have to start trusting in themselves."

"And did you learn to trust in yourself?"

"It took a long time. There were many successes and even more failures, but in the end I started to learn that if I did what I thought was best for myself it ultimately turned out to be the best for everyone concerned."

"Very good."

"The world is full of extraordinary people who think that they can only live ordinary lives. They don't realize that they can each make their lives extraordinary."

"And how would they go about doing that?"

"By saying yes to life, by saying yes to their dreams. Hey, just look what happened to me."

"Yes, We did."

"So, tell me. Did I accomplish what I set out to do? Do you think the people listened to what I was trying to tell them this time?"

"Only time will tell."

"Yes, but imagine if they did. Just imagine!"

About Samarah

Born in the Midwest, Samarah states that from her earliest moments she could hear angels and guides speaking to her. She said it was like an ever-present radio, sometimes soft, other times louder, yet always available.

As an adult Samarah found a career first as a high school English teacher and then as a real estate broker, all the while still connected to her inner world. She became a Usui Reiki master and studied with a variety of spiritual teachers like Ram Dass and Wayne Dyer. In 1979 she became a certified Director of Psychodrama, a field of psychology developed by J.L. Moreno in which group dynamics and drama are used to explore and heal traumas and dysfunctional patterns.

For the last eleven years Samarah has been channeling the loving wisdom of Masters from the Realms of Light. She has traveled internationally as an ordained Madonna Minister, channeling Mother Mary at the Chalice Well in Glastonbury, amidst the trees and green of Scotland's Findhorn and at gatherings large and small from Maine to California.

Samarah found that during her meditations she was able to make contact with a variety of angelic beings. For about ten months she had been "conversing" with Archangel Gabriel. She is transcribing his messages and was working toward a book to be entitled "The Gabriel Letters." One afternoon in her home in Scottsdale, Arizona during a meditation, visualizing each color of the chakras, a meditation she had done for years, she felt something different. She felt a thick bluish cloud of light and a powerful and very large energy in the room. She recalls bowing her head to this powerful presence and asking telepathically, "Who are you?" and a sweet clear voice answered, "Many call me Mary." Samarah replied, "How can I be of service to you?" and this powerful presence simply replied, "Will you BE with me?" Not knowing in that moment what her commitment would mean, everything in Samarah simply replied, "Yes."

Samarah felt Mary's presence with her for a while that afternoon. Nothing else was said. Then, she was gone. Each day for the next eleven days she came in the afternoon between two and four and would visit with Samarah. Rarely speaking, she would just "be" with her.

Not knowing what she would say to those who questioned her or wanted to share her experience, Samarah told no one. She treasured and savored the experience and felt a kind of peace that she could not explain. She felt loved unconditionally. After the first two weeks, Mary came at odd hours and different times and now began to "speak" to Samarah and urged her to write down her messages. At first she wrote them down for herself but as the work increased in volume and in urgency, Samarah chose a few friends and invited them to come and hear Mother Mary speak through her. She was more comfortable writing what the voice told her but there came a time when she knew that she was simply to get out of the way and Mother Mary would speak.

Samarah understandably had many doubts and fears. What would her friends think? Was she crazy? If word got out would there be dozens of people camped out on her lawn? Samarah brought these fears to Mother Mary and she asked, "What is it that you would create?" Samarah's reply was that she would choose to be a clear channel for Mary's information and that people could respond to the messages, not to her, for she was simply the vehicle. And Mary said, "Then so it will be."

That first night in 1997, Samarah sat in her living room with six friends and a tape recorder. She told them that this was simply an experience and that they were free to doubt or question anything that was said. Samarah felt protective of Her and vulnerable to what would come. So began the communications and conversations with Mother Mary that continue to this day.

Samarah feels that Mary is here to teach us about love and believes that she continues to come because we are still learning what love is. Samarah states that her path is to offer what she hears and feels as the voice of Blessed Mother Mary. She offers it to us as information for our journey. She also states that if it fills us with peace and brings us comfort, she rejoices. If it is not for you then she rejoices in your knowing what is best for you. Her wish is that we each find what brings us closer to God, that we all may create a world of peace and harmony.

You can contact Samarah on her website: www.channelmary.com